By profession **Stewart Whyte** is a researcher and internationally published author of how-to books with a particular focus on getting into the bed & breakfast/fa   y business. In 2007, he wrote the curriculum for two self-paced onli   rses for the Bed & Breakfast Institute, which are currently marketed   en countries. Well known as an authority on the B&B industry, he has be   id ting courses and lectures for the last twenty years, and has been i   v   on both radio and TV. Stewart often consults with govern   ments on compliancy issues in relation to bed & breakfasts.

Other titles

How To Make Money from Your Home

Do It Yourself Bookkeeping for Small Businesses

Quick Wins in Sales and Marketing

The Small Business Start-up Workbook

Start and Run a Business from Home

How to Start and Run a B&B

4th Edition

Stewart Whyte

....

A How To Book

ROBINSON

First published in Great Britain in 2018
by Robinson

10 9 8 7 6 5 4 3 2 1

Important Note
The material contained in this book is set out
for general guidance and does not
deal with any particular and personal
circumstances. Laws and regulations are
complex and liable to change, and readers
should check the current position with
relevant authorities before making individual
arrangements and where necessary
take appropriate advice.

A CIP catalogue record for this book
is available from the British Library.

ISBN: 978-1-47214-059-3

Typeset in Great Britain by
Mousemat Design Limited

Printed and bound in Great Britain by
CPI Group (UK), Croydon CR0 4YY

Papers used by Robinson are from well-
managed forests and other sustainable sources

MIX
Paper from
responsible sources
FSC® C104740

Robinson
An imprint of
Little, Brown Book Group
Carmelite House
50 Victoria Embankment
London EC4Y 0DZ

An Hachette UK Company
www.hachette.co.uk

www.littlebrown.co.uk

How To Books are published by Robinson,
an imprint of Little, Brown Book Group.
We welcome proposals from authors who
have first-hand experience of their
subjects. Please set out the aims of your
book, its target market and its suggested
contents in an email to
Nikki.Read@howtobooks.co.uk

To invite someone to be our guest
Is to undertake responsibility for
Their happiness all the time that
They are under our roof.

Jean Anthelme Brillat-Savarin (1755–1826)
Author, epicure, raconteur

Contents

Acknowledgements

This book would not be as comprehensive without the wonderful contribution of the following people and organisations:

Gideon Stanley from Gracesoft.com; Warren Whyte for his advice on banking procedures; Wal Reynolds for his input in the feasibility and business-plan sections; Ryan Insurance Group for their advice on business insurance for B&B operators, and Ceneta Insurance Services for their advice on public/private insurance cover.

Over the years I have kept updated on tourist statistics and trends as published by the world's leading research houses and tourism authorities, and it's these people and institutions that I want to congratulate. The tourist industry could not function without their advice.

I also wish to thank Suellen Harwood for her common-sense approach on how to run a successful bed & breakfast business.

I would like to thank all of the bed & breakfast owners for their advice and tips that newcomers in the industry will find invaluable.

Until next time,

Stewart

Preface

The growth in popularity of visitors choosing to stay in home-hosted accommodation is a success story in most parts of the world. This has been mostly brought about by the impact of international reservation platforms, which use the internet to promote bed & breakfast accommodation.

In studying the property types, and identifying the main reason why people list their properties with the large reservation platforms, one finds that there is now a clear distinction between the traditional bed & breakfast and the short-let, part-time operator. The latter are mainly made up of those in it for a quick and often short-term return, and who have listed their property on the likes of Airbnb.

The obvious two categories are:

1. Short-let, part-time hosts, many of whom are already restricted on the number of days in a year that they will be allowed to trade and the predicted high compliance costs that will be imposed on them by the regulators. This may mean that their involvement in this business is no longer viable.
2. The more traditional bed & breakfasts that abide by local government regulations and can, if they choose, trade 365 days a year. It is also noticed that this category tends to be more professional than the majority of short-let, part-time operators. It should be noted that many are also listed with the international reservation platforms and are doing very well.

Never before have regulators been so concerned with the large number of property owners who have taken their house out of the rental market and subsequently put a lot of pressure on property availability and rental prices.

There is also a backlash from bed & breakfast owners who abide by the rules, but find that the next-door neighbour has not. This is the reason why change is inevitable in order to bring some sanity into the industry.

To that end, this book is an ideal read for those who now want to be a more professional host, whether it is full-time or part-time, and want to make real money, and for those who want to start a home-based business.

So, to meet demand and substantiate the bed & breakfast's place in the tourism industry, there is a growing need for increased knowledge and professionalism among bed & breakfast operators. To assist you in your endeavour, a feasibility study has been included in this international edition, along with a business-plan example.

Current trends show that changes in the workplace could be one of the main contributors to the high level of interest in becoming a bed & breakfast operator. Another influential factor is the continuing growth of the short-break holiday market. Those who take short-break holidays historically prefer this form of accommodation.

It is important to remember, however, that knowledge is not an end in itself. You must use the knowledge gained from this publication as a resource and stepping stone to achieve your goals and fulfil your aspirations.

The main message is that the research you need to do to make your B&B a success must be personal to you and your market.

How to Start and Run a B&B has been researched and written by someone who has carefully studied the practicalities and the needs of people who are either in the industry or wishing to enter it.

In constructing this book, I have tried to avoid duplication of material that exists in other training manuals and how-to publications, preferring to concentrate on that which is directly applicable to the industry. I have gathered up-to-date information from industry leaders and practitioners internationally to give the reader a source of information that reflects the practicalities and requirements necessary for the successful bed & breakfast operator.

All issues covered in this book are significant, but professionalism is the most important. This book will reinforce the need to seek professional advice in the early stages of your venture and give you an insight into the level of professionalism you need to consider in order to be a success in this business.

Good luck on your venture!

Stewart Whyte

Introduction

How to Start and Run a B&B is divided into two main sections for easy access. Part One is designed for you to discover if you, your partner, your family, your home and your bank balance are ready to enter this industry. It will also allow you to decide what level of commitment you are prepared to make to this venture: full-time/weekends/breakfasts only/full board, etc. We also show you how to do a feasibility study that tests the viability of your commercial proposition before you start spending money and time on it.

If you have decided that operating a bed & breakfast is your dream for a better future then Part Two will be an introduction to the daily issues that confront bed & breakfast operators, and will outline how to run a bed & breakfast efficiently and successfully. Included at the end of this section are the guidelines to completing your own business plan.

Throughout this book you will find two symbols. The single symbol 🏠 is applicable to all operators, but in particular to those whose commitment to the enterprise is on a very small scale (perhaps one or two bedrooms, and not the only source of income). The double symbol 🏠🏠 is for those whose enterprise (i.e. guesthouse) is on a larger scale and who need it to contribute substantially to the household income.

The following are questions you might like to ask yourself before you read any further. As you progress through the book you may like to return to this page to see how your ideas on what it takes to run a successful bed & breakfast have altered.

- *What parts of my character make me a perfect host or hostess?*
- *What implications do I think that owning and operating a bed & breakfast will have on my personal life?*
- *Who will be my target market?*
- *What facilities do I already have?*
- *What additional facilities do I think I will need to provide or acquire?*
- *What financial investment do I think will be needed to start the venture?*
- *Do I have this amount of finance available?*

- *If not, where do I expect it will come from?*
- *Who do I expect to be my customers?*
- *Why will they come to my bed & breakfast rather than some other type of accommodation?*
- *How will my potential customers hear about my bed & breakfast?*
- *Will I advertise? If so, where will I advertise?*
- *How much do I intend to charge?*
- *What factors did I look at to reach this figure?*
- *What factors will influence whether my establishment makes a profit or loss?*
- *What legal obligations do I have?*
- *What are the main skills needed to run a successful bed & breakfast?*
- *What are my main skills?*
- *What kinds of additional help will I require?*
- *Where will this help come from?*
- *How much do I know about employing people?*
- *When do I intend to begin accommodating guests?*
- *What factors are most likely to inhibit me?*
- *What will my feasibility study contain and does it make sense?*

Having taken stock of your current expectations and knowledge, we will begin looking into the whos, whats, whys and wherefores of operating a successful bed & breakfast or guesthouse no matter where in the world you are located.

Part One

Preparing to Enter the B&B Business

1 It's Up to You

So, you want to run a bed & breakfast! WHY? This is very possibly the most important question you will ask yourself as you read this book.

WHY? Is it because you have had some part-time experience hosting people by listing your property with Airbnb or similar international reservation platforms, and now want to be a full-time host and become a bed & breakfast owner? Is it because you have stayed in a few over the years and it seems such a nice way to earn a living? Is it because you went away for the weekend and saw this gorgeous period or historic homestead and it was only a small amount of money and it would be such fun to do up, and hadn't you both talked about making a sea-change decision and moving out of the city? Is it because you really like to cook, and have always loved it when your best friends or family visit you from distant places? Is it because you think it will be a way to make your fortune?

There are many different reasons people enter the bed & breakfast market and you need to think clearly about why it is that you wish to enter it. Because, make no mistake about it, the difference between a good and bad B&B is you, the host. Why you are embarking on this adventure matters, because you need to create a business plan that will match the goals you have for your bed & breakfast. Be prepared to discover that running a B&B may not achieve those goals for you.

TIP
Be prepared to roll up your sleeves past your elbows!

The harsh news first: very few B&Bs support their owners in the first few years. And second: if you start with two guest bedrooms your earning capacity will be limited.

The main reasons for failure are over-capitalising on the part of the owners, and the management process of the property itself. Burnout can also be a significant factor in the pursuit of a lifestyle change.

There is a difference between spending on essentials, such as en-suites in each guest bedroom, which are rapidly becoming a necessity, and filling your house with expensive antiques, which will not always make a guest decide to stay with you or return.

A flair for redecorating does not necessarily make you a good host. Neither does enjoying entertaining friends and family. Running a bed & breakfast is a twenty-four-hour commitment. You need to be prepared to 'entertain' at all hours of the day and night and have your private life disturbed, and in some case share your personal space with strangers. This can be difficult but, if you are to be a successful host, the spirit of giving must be embraced twenty-four hours a day. This spirit should inhabit every exchange, every phone call, every letter or email. To be a successful host you need to LOVE PEOPLE and be prepared to share your life and home with them. But, never forget quality time for yourself and your family.

It's all about personality

As you work through this book you are going to be asked a lot of questions. Now is the time to start a notebook to record the answers to all the questions asked of you. This will be invaluable in determining your market and creating your feasibility study. At the same time, start a folder for filing all the information you will need to collect prior to starting your B&B.

> **TIP**
> Identify your target market prior to deciding whether your family is ready and your property is suitable.

Do I have the type of personality that will make me a wonderful host? Write down your answers and refer to them later when evaluating whether you are the right kind of person to run a bed & breakfast.

Do I like people? This is very important. You can't just think that people are just OK when you enter the B&B industry. You need to genuinely like people and be interested in them. You have to love individuals and the idiosyncrasies that come with individualism.

Am I prepared to do almost anything to make my guests feel important and spoiled? This is the essence of a good host.

Will I enjoy guests, who are in effect strangers, wandering in and out of my home, treating it as if it were their own? When you are living in the same house as your guests, privacy will become a thing of the past.

Am I willing to be available twenty-four hours a day? Guests and potential guests have the habit of calling, arriving or wanting your help at the most inopportune times. You need to be prepared to drop whatever it is you are doing and provide service with a smile.

Am I going to be able to live with a difficult person over the whole time of their visit? And will I be able to cope with this person in my home? People can be difficult and if you don't have the patience of a saint you may find this life hard.

Can I accept the old adage that the customer is always right? Guests, or potential guests, may be demanding and want things that are unreasonable. Meeting some of their needs will be impossible. However, you must be prepared to compromise and try to make your guests happy whenever possible, even when it's against your better judgement. You can't afford to be Basil Fawlty! Word of mouth is the key here: use it as a marketing tool. Your guests' stay should be of such high quality that they act as your ambassadors, spreading the good news of your B&B.

Are my partner and family as equally committed to this lifestyle choice as I am? Without passion on all sides you are destined for failure, early burnout or, at worst, relationship difficulties.

> **TIP**
>
> If you can't find it in your heart to make a grumpy person smile, keep out of the people business.

Am I dedicated housekeeper? Untidiness just won't do as a bed & breakfast operator. You need to be a fastidious housekeeper. Do you enjoy vacuuming every day? Do you notice if something is out of place? Do your friends call you a perfectionist? Good.

These are the perfect qualities for a B&B host, where near enough is never good enough.

The dream of working for yourself

Being your own boss can be a great way to earn a living. Let's face it, most of us have had this dream. Being able to throw our job in and to go out on our own. Make our mark. Keep the profits for ourselves. And for many, that is where it stays – a dream. However, a few of us decide to take the plunge and whether we are successful in our endeavour primarily depends on two things: our motivation for entering the business to begin with, and our preparedness for entering the business at that time.

Successful small-business operators have chosen to work for themselves for positive reasons: not because they hate what they are leaving behind, but because they are excited about creating something for the future – including profits.

They often are extremely motivated and self-disciplined. Not only does your goal need to be uppermost in your mind when opening your own business, you must have the discipline to divide work from your private life – particularly when your business is in your home. Successful small-business people thrive away from the constraints of an employer.

Financial goals are also an important focus for the successful small-business owner. Your business plan needs to clearly set out the financial goals for your business with strategies to help you reach them. The most successful small-business people have a financial and career goal that is unable to be satisfied by working for someone else.

You also need to realise you are leaving the world of the secure pay packet. Gone forever are the hidden financial benefits of working for a wage or salary. It is now all up to you. You need to feel comfortable about this and could consider consulting a financial planner for advice about managing your financial future.

The financial reality

The bad news is that most small businesses fail during the first three years. The main reason for this is lack of planning by the owner, both at the set-up stage and ongoing. Entering the ranks for the wrong reason to begin with exacerbates this.

The worst reasons to go into business for yourself are: no one else will employ you; you want flexible working hours with more time to play than work; and you think that all it takes to make a fortune in your own business is a good idea. This last statement is the biggest misconception.

The best ideas in the world won't work if you don't plan to succeed – and have the ability to convince everyone else that your idea *is* a good idea. The reasons most often cited for failure in small businesses are:

- a lack of business and/or management experience;
- inadequate, inaccurate or non-existent financial records;
- taking too much money from the business for personal use; and
- lack of adequate seed and working capital.

A solid business plan will help prevent you becoming another statistic. We all know about the bottom line, but the top line, that is research, is equally important.

Thorough research in the early stages of your venture makes you less likely to fail in the long run.

Consider both the advantages and disadvantages of being your own boss. There is no doubt that it will place some stresses on your lifestyle and relationships in the first few years while you establish a pattern.

Bonuses can be satisfaction, management autonomy and building financial independence. Negatives can be sporadic income, long and irregular hours, competition, possible failure and relationship difficulties.

Money in the bank

Unless you are going into bed & breakfast as a hobby or interest, money could be a problem for the first few years.

Many B&B operators make the mistake of thinking that holidaymakers are just waiting for them to open their doors and then they will be booked up for months. This doesn't always happen. B&Bs, for the most part, are built on word of mouth and word of mouth takes time to gather momentum. In today's business environment, a good website will be needed, particularly if you are not listed with a reservation platform, and this will also take time to gather momentum.

You need to have a plan for how you will survive financially until you build a clientele. How much money do you have in the bank? How long can you survive with your outgoings outweighing your income? Do you fully own your property? That is the most comfortable financial option. Do you or your partner plan to supplement your income with a second job?

Think about these questions and try to put together a *financial contingency plan* allowing for a slow flow of guests at first.

A look in the mirror

Before we go any further, look in the mirror. Hard. Then ask yourself the following questions. An *honest* answer to these questions will help you decide whether you are the right person to enter the B&B market and will help to reduce the potential for failure.

- *Am I self-driven?* When you work for yourself you need to be able to motivate yourself.
- *Am I organised?* Running a business by yourself or with a partner needs systematic planning.

- *Do both my partner and I share the right temperament to be B&B hosts?* Are you both friendly, relaxed, organised and charming?
- *Am I a problem solver or do I tend to become indecisive when faced with a lot of problems or questions?* Running a business requires constant decision-making and the ability to prevent a crisis.
- *Am I confident, without being overbearing?* You need to be able to sell your business to banks, customers, the media, etc. The essence of a good B&B operator is warmth of personality: you need to have the ability to attract people to you, not distance them from you.
- *Am I willing to take advice and learn from others?* Successful business people are always on the lookout for good ideas and advice. They then take the best of this and mould it into their own business. They work on their business, not in it.
- *Am I prepared to learn the skills needed to run a business?* This takes time and effort.
- *Am I experienced in leading people, and am I prepared to learn?* Owning a business often requires you to hire, motivate and, in the worst cases, dismiss staff. This takes a certain skill.
- *Do I have the ability to set clear and attainable goals?* You need a business plan that is achievable otherwise you are setting yourself up for disappointment.
- *Do I have the skills of negotiation?* Owning your own business will require the forming of relationships with other business people around you. In times of conflict, you need to be able to negotiate win-win agreements with all parties concerned.
- *Can I handle stress?* If heavy traffic or queues worry you, this is nothing to the stress you may experience when you have a cash-flow problem – an all too common problem when operating a small business.
- *Do I have strong communication skills?* Being a host requires the attributes of a perfect personality. You need to be naturally pleasant and agreeable. Those of you who are moody will very likely not find this way of life to your liking. You need to be able to make conversation while avoiding political or religious topics, or other discussion minefields. You need to be patient and tolerant and know the difference between making polite conversation and becoming a nuisance.

A family affair

TIP
Before going into the bed & breakfast business, stay in a few yourself so as to better understand what the host has to cope with.

Operating a bed & breakfast with a family means that not only should you have the right personality for hosting guests, but so should the other members of your family.

Success is dependent on an equal commitment from everybody concerned. Living on the premises of your business can be distracting enough for an individual – for those of you with a family this disruption can be tenfold.

It is not impossible for you both to run a successful B&B and raise a family on the same premises, but it does require family cooperation and understanding.

You should factor into your business plan contingencies that should ensure the success of your business without disrupting your family's happiness. You might want to consider having a defined letting period to protect your family's privacy. For example, you might only let rooms four nights a week or forty weeks a year, taking your break in the low season. This limitation will, however, affect your income projections, so you must factor this into your feasibility study or business plan.

Consider having a separate annex for your family so that family life is separated from your business life.

Organise time out for you and your family to spend away from your 'office'. No one wants to spend 365 days a year, 24 hours a day at his or her workplace.

If you have children living at home, then three nights and four days of having guests may be the maximum – if you want to retain family unity.

Have a friend or colleague who can be available to step in and act as a paid caretaker of your business should you need to get away or if you are unwell.

Factor in time to discuss and explain to your children why you are entering this business and what the consequences may be for them. Their cooperation will be directly proportional to their level of understanding.

Explain to your children that they are to be polite and friendly to guests at all times, and not to impose on them unless asked.

Remember many couples who frequent B&Bs come to escape their children – they won't really want to spend time with yours. If your children are very young, you should really consider whether now is the right time for you to open your B&B. Raising very young children and running a B&B are both physically and emotionally draining. Trying to juggle both could see you lose your sense of balance.

The other consideration of running a B&B with children at home is that they will want to spend time with you when they are at home, which is primarily at weekends. Weekends, however, are often your busiest trading period. You will need to balance these two claims on your time.

Equal commitment within your family structure is crucial. Tension between family members becomes palpable and your guests will feel it. This will be uncomfortable for all concerned and will not result in return visits.

Going it alone

Is it possible to do this without a family? It certainly is – more and more bed & breakfasts are being run by single people. In some respects, you may find this way of life easier than those with a family or an uncommitted partner, as you know you are committed to your business and will ensure that everything is as it should be.

> **TIP**
> Be mindful of the impact running a bed & breakfast has on family life, especially if your children still live at home. Life as you know it will never be the same.

The only disadvantages are time-out periods – which you will need if you are to be successful. Ensure that you have time out from the business to do other things you enjoy. If you have always wanted to do drawing classes, do them.

If you want to go on holidays, think of hiring an experienced couple to mind your operation while you are away – there are a number of professionals who specialise in this. Have your phone calls linked to your mobile and participate in life.

> **TIP**
> One of the nice things about bed & breakfast is the flexibility of being able to decide when to have guests.

The other thing is not to over-host your guests – or use them to stave off loneliness. As a good B&B host you should know when your guests want your company and when they do not. This is where your people skills will come in.

It's time

So, you are comfortable that you have the right personality to make a success of the bed & breakfast business.

It's now time to get a better appreciation of the tourist trends as they apply to your country. This is important information to know because it can influence future decisions.

2 Who Is Your Market?

Before deciding exactly whom you are going to target for your bed & breakfast, it is a good idea to know something about tourism in your country. This is one of the largest industries in the world and you want to get it right, so it is important to monitor travel trends on a regular basis.

Knowing the number of domestic travellers and international visitors coming into your area on an annual or seasonal basis enables you to better plan for likely demand. Using this information, you can start developing your market strategy to attract your share of the tourist spend in your area (see Chapter 13).

Understanding the international market

The following is a snapshot of tourism statistics and predictions that indicate the size of the global tourism market. (Given that statistics change on a regular basis, we suggest you keep yourself up to date by researching tourism trends, using the internet.)

According to the United Nations World Tourism Organization's *UNWTO Tourism Highlights* (2016 edition), the number of international tourist arrivals (overnight visitors) in 2015 increased by 4.6 per cent to reach a total of 1186 million worldwide, an increase of 52 million over the previous year. It was the sixth consecutive year of above-average growth in international tourism following the 2009 global economic crisis.

Tourism flows were influenced by three major factors in 2015: the unusually strong exchange-rate fluctuations, the decline in the price of oil and other commodities, and increased global concern about safety and security.

By UNWTO region, the Americas and Asia and the Pacific both recorded close to 6 per cent growth in international tourist arrivals, with Europe, the world's most visited region, recording 5 per cent. Arrivals in the Middle East increased by 2 per cent, while in Africa they declined by 3 per cent, mostly due to weak results in North Africa. International tourism receipts grew by 4.4 per cent in real terms (taking into account exchange-rate fluctuations and inflation) with total earnings in the destinations estimated at US$1260 billion worldwide in 2015 (1136 billion euros).

International tourist arrivals worldwide are expected to increase by 3.3 per cent a year between 2010 and 2030 to reach 1.8 billion by 2030, according to UNWTO's long-term forecast report, *Tourism Towards 2030*. Between 2010 and 2030, arrivals in emerging destinations (+4.4 per cent a year) are expected to increase at twice the rate of those in advanced economies (+2.2 per cent a year). The market share of emerging economies increased from 30 per cent in 1980 to 45 per cent in 2015, and is expected to reach 57 per cent by 2030, equivalent to over one billion international tourist arrivals.

Notes

In summary, global trends indicate that people travelling in the future will take more 'short-break holidays' than ever before.

The short-break market trend is due to several different factors, among them the trickle-down effect of changes in the workplace. Visitors will often stay in more than one location in the same or nearby countries rather than be confined to one location. They will be better educated and more affluent, with high expectations of customer service and value for money.

> **TIP**
> Be sure you read up on their country of origin when your guests are from overseas.

The domestic market

The number of domestic trips undertaken by the general public is projected to expand in the future. Again, due to changes in the workplace, people will take more short breaks than ever before. The ease with which the travelling public can now book accommodation online with the international reservation platforms, for example Airbnb, is driving this demand.

Stress in the workplace is already starting to produce a knock-on effect on personal relationships and, subsequently, people will take more time out with their loved ones if only to resolve any rifts that might be emerging.

Holiday patterns are starting to change. Where in the past, holiday-makers predominately took elongated weekends, they are now finding that someone in their family may be employed on a part-time basis during the weekend, so they will have to take some of their break during the week. For the future, many accommodation houses will start to notice more evenness throughout the week as people take breaks to fit in with a deregulated workplace.

Short-break holidays

The short-break market has become increasingly significant in recent years with current tourism trends throughout the world moving in favour of one- to three-night breaks rather than fortnightly holidays. Here is what some tourism bodies have to say:

The traditional two-week summer holiday is becoming less important for many people. There are thought to be a number of social trends affecting the marketplace, including, for example: the 'time-squeeze' phenomenon – many people feel they have shorter windows of time in which to take holidays; household size is falling – people have more to spend and are less constrained by school holidays; an ageing population – with more time to take more breaks.

These social trends have already changed the nature of tourism.

The tourism statistics above are a guide only, but they will assist you in matching the tourist size by volume and expenditure against the region where you wish to establish a bed & breakfast.

All tourist authorities have their own websites where you can gather meaningful information to help you do your homework.

3 Who Is Your Customer?

This chapter is all about having you focus on who you believe will be your customer. Why do you need to work this out now? Before you decide where you buy, what you are going to buy or what renovations you will need to convert your existing property, you must know if the market – or customer base – can support your endeavour.

Getting your facts straight

So, how do you go about finding the size of your potential market? If you have not been involved in tourism before, then you will have a limited idea as to why people come into your area or, for that matter, what your geographical location has to offer.

The starting point is to source where reliable information can be gathered on key issues such as location, costs, staff requirements, time constraints and a whole host of operating details. At this stage, potential bed & breakfast operators need answers; that is, facts and details upon which they can build a comprehensive picture of their proposed operation, the possible market, the methods of operation, etc. They need to undertake research to give them a realistic understanding of their prospective business.

Your bed & breakfast will not appeal to everybody. You should be identifying the type of guests you want to attract; that is, your preferred *target market.*

What type of guests would you like to attract to your B&B? The choice is yours – you should at this early stage make this decision. Would you prefer to be servicing the top end of the market or the general holidaymaker? Would you feel more comfortable with corporate clients or with family groups or groups of friends? Your choice of target market will be a vital factor in influencing your decision on where to locate and how to design your premises.

If, on the other hand, you decide to use your existing dwelling with modifications, then you must determine what type of guest your bed & breakfast will attract.

The following table contains ten categories of target guests to help you to identify your prime market group and also your preference towards two subsidiary groups, listed in order. Socioeconomic considerations should apply in all categories, as should preferred age brackets.

TARGET MARKET OPTIONS

Market Segment	Prime Market	Subsidiary Market 1	Subsidiary Market 2
Affluent guests			
Couples			
Singles			
Families			
Corporate			
Guests with a disability			
Budget market			
Groups			
Gay/Lesbian			
Other: Guests with pets, etc.			

Having identified your preferred market groups (this can also indicate age and income), you can now decide whether you are looking at a purely 'commercial venture' or if you are considering a 'lifestyle adjustment' still using your existing dwelling. You have two clear options!

1. A commercial venture is a standalone business where the income is your prime source of revenue.
2. A lifestyle adjustment is when you decide to get into bed & breakfast as a means of generating a top-up or secondary income and as a sea-change option. This may well become a prime income source in the future.

Once your decision has been made as to what type of bed & breakfast business you want to run, we suggest a visit to your local tourist information centre to get the most recent facts and figures on how many visitors your preferred area attracts per year. In doing so, you will find out how old they are, what they do, how long they stay, and what and why they are visiting. They should also be able to advise you how many other accommodation suppliers are in your area, their average occupancy rate and any other information regarding the visitors to your area, including the type of holidays and accommodation people are choosing. You should be able to ascertain the trends that are occurring. If you notice discrepancies when comparing the data collected, you might be able to bridge any gaps.

Fast facts

The following are some facts that will help to put the information you are seeking into some context. It could also be of some assistance with various sections of your *feasibility study* or *business plan.*

Research indicates that over the next five years, the domestic market will continue to take more short-break holidays, usually two nights and three days, with more frequency than ever before. Many people surveyed said they would be undertaking this break with their partner, but without children. Fifty per cent said this break would be in their own country.

Many more women are travelling for both leisure and business as their roles in the workplace become more significant.

Progressively, more people will use the internet to book holidays and, believe it, they will often be last-minute bookings after destinations and prices have been compared. They will be seeking new experiences and a better understanding of the culture in the areas visited. More visitors are choosing their destinations based on their specific interests, for example, researching family history.

There are a few other things of which you should be aware. As we know, the world is constantly changing. Rapid and geographically unbalanced economic growth has been predicted to come to an end in the middle of this century. Over this period, the world is predicted to move from the present situation of income inequality, with low average wages, to reasonable income equality, with much higher average income.

Between now and 2050 the world's income is forecast to increase tenfold. The largest economies will be in Asia. However, among the ten biggest economies, per capita income is expected to remain highest in the United States.

The key demographic development is the death rate. If, as some people maintain, average life expectancy will rise to about a hundred years, the world's population may stabilize at approximately ten billion. However, if medical causes of death are lessened by medical progress, then world population may pass ten billion, and keep rising for some time, at about one billion per decade.

People are living longer. And there are far more of them. This means two things for you.

1. Retired people need something to supplement their income in their golden years – which in effect could last for thirty to forty years.
2. And they will want somewhere to go on a short-break holiday within a two- to three-hour driving distance from their home, bed & breakfasts being a favoured accommodation choice.

It is projected that by the year 2020, more than 40 per cent of the workforce could be employed on a part-time basis. This means that those of us who, for the future, want to earn the same income that we currently enjoy, will need to have two or three part-time jobs. These won't necessarily be in the same industry. People will have to up-skill in order to get these jobs. To be one of the approximately 50 per cent still employed full-time you will need to be highly skilled and trained and be willing to further your education at every opportunity.

Rather than face this ultra-competitive job market, many older (and some younger) people are becoming consultants or contractors. Instead of falling into the 1980s trap of renting an expensive office in a good suburb, however, they are working out of their high-tech office at home. B&Bs are a great way to help supplement the peaks and troughs of a consultancy business, if your property is in a suitable location.

We have found that 75 per cent of people who are exploring the idea of entering the bed & breakfast market are corporate workers doing so as a financial contingency plan for their future. The other 25 per cent do so for emotional reasons. Bed & breakfasts are a soft financial risk. You may own your own home. If you don't get a lot of bookings you still own your home – you haven't lost your financial shirt.

The hours spent by many retailers who are out of their home and in their shop increases every year, as consumers want to shop when they are not working. Remember, we are all working longer hours.

Which brings us to another point in the B&B's favour.

Traditionally people worked nine to five, Monday to Friday. If you owned a bed & breakfast that focused on the domestic market, then your business was restricted, primarily, to weekends. With the increase of flexible working hours and the decrease of the mid-year, two- to three-week holiday, more people are choosing several short holiday breaks throughout the year, often midweek, or as an adjunct to their weekend.

It is estimated that 39 per cent of people had not taken all their accrued holidays in the past year; 14 per cent of these people had not taken any leave in the past year, with more than a quarter not having had a holiday for more than two years. Job-security concerns are being touted as the likely reason for this, the trend being that people are much more comfortable having a short-break holiday than leaving their office for extended periods. Employers and governments are being pressured into encouraging their employees to take full leave entitlements.

> **TIP**
>
> Keep yourself up to date with the short-break holiday trends. This market segment is already gathering pace.

It has been estimated that by the year 2023 there will be 4.5 billion people in the middle-income group, with three out of five being Asian.

Capturing your target market

So how can you capture this market? Make no mistake about it – to be a success at bed & breakfast you need to capture it. Bed & breakfasts in cities are becoming a more and more attractive option. Being close to a business district is becoming a desirable location. There needs to be a reason to go to your area, something to do as well as rest.

Are you near a national park and walking tracks? Close to a tourist area, the Lake District, Yellowstone, the Blue Mountains, Tongariro National Park, Banff National Park, Kruger National Park, Loch Ness or the southern Irish coast? Are you in a popular country town, Keswick, Maitland, Fielding, Coffee Bay, St Andrews-by-the-Sea? Are you in a high-density commercial area? These are the factors you need to consider before you start.

If you want to attract a particular type of person, for example, executives visiting your city for conferences, make sure that they will feel at home with you and your partner or family. Ideally, your target market should be people like you or who like the things you like. In the long run, your business will be a greater success.

You also need to ensure that your proposed customers come into your area in reasonable numbers. Have you checked that they are coming to your area now?

If you want to attract *business* or *corporate clients* you will need to look at your local community and its market potential. Are companies attracted to your area for conferences? Is your local council doing a lot to attract businesses to relocate to your area? You need to ensure your council and tourist office understand the service you can provide by, for example, being able to show these visitors the 'real' experience of your community.

Have you thought about academics? Does your town have a *university* or a *tertiary college*? Introduce yourself to the person responsible for booking the accommodation for these visitors, send them your promotional literature and invite them to come and stay for a night. If they enjoy their stay, they are more likely to book with you.

If, like many B&Bs, you see your market as *overseas guests*, you need to investigate why tourists are attracted to your area. Is it the local markets? Historic areas or the pubs? While determining this, visit your tourist centre for their research on visitor numbers.

You also need to find out the average age of the people visiting your area. This information will help you to determine the facilities you need to provide to attract this market. It also helps you to spend your promotional budget wisely.

Niche markets

This brings us to niche markets. Within the tourist sector you may want to specialise in a particular type of tourist, usually a person who is attracted specifically to your area, or *shares your interest or passion*. Some examples of this are fishermen, hikers, birdwatchers, history buffs and people wanting a romantic getaway.

To target a particular niche, you may need to consider the following:

- *That you have particular knowledge of that market yourself.* If your area is known for its fauna and flora and you intend to exploit this market, you will need to know about this yourself. It would help if you had contact with a naturalist or a ranger, who could give guided walks or hold weekend workshops for visitors.

- *You may need to supply special facilities.* If your passion is cooking and you are going to run a creative cooking school, you may need to change the layout of your kitchen in order to support this.

If your niche is going to be trout fishermen you may want to consider putting up attractive photos of local fishing spots in your hallway or displaying a mounted trophy. A word of caution here. Don't go overboard, as you don't want to put off other guests. A few details here and there will provide a conversation point.

Promotion

You need to launch your entry into the market with advertising and editorial in appropriate journals. Offer influential people and decision-makers within your niche community a weekend away at your bed & breakfast. It is positive word of mouth that will assist in promoting your speciality.

There are major groups that people can target with great success. We will discuss them now in detail.

The corporate market

Some B&B operators capture the corporate market midweek and the leisure market during the weekend. If you have travelled extensively on business then many of you would agree that the part you detest is dining by yourself! Bed & breakfasts can supply the corporate traveller with a degree of normality during their trip.

Some larger bed & breakfasts and guest-houses target corporate business to stage strategy meetings at their establishment. To do this successfully you need the right facilities: a meeting room, computers for PowerPoint demonstrations and emails, white boards, markers, photocopiers, full catering facilities, etc. For larger establishments, this can be quite lucrative. Your guests will definitely want to check their email so wi-fi would be useful.

TIP
Real-estate agents and community organisations such as Rotary Clubs and Lions Clubs are a good source to access the corporate market.

Single travellers

There are many single people who only talk to people at work; they go home by themselves, to themselves. They need a holiday too, even if it is just to meet and talk to others.

Single travellers often want to know the real heart of a city or town and meeting the locals is part of that. What better way to meet the locals than to stay in their home? You need to be centrally located and close to transport.

You will not win any points if your guest needs to travel up poorly lit, suburban streets to reach the local bus stop or train station.

Please do single travellers a favour and don't banish them to your smallest, dingiest room. Remember that the single traveller is paying more per head than your average couple, and they are eating less, and using less electricity and hot water. Treat them well and they will return the favour, recommending you to other single travellers.

Women travellers

The single female traveller is an ever-growing market – both as part of work and as part of adventure. Some women, however, feel uncomfortable sitting by themselves having dinner. If they go to a restaurant alone they are in danger of attracting unwanted attention from the opposite sex, or they feel trapped in their room if they order room service. Bed & breakfasts are a great antidote to this, particularly those that offer the option of an evening meal.

For the single woman, the bed & breakfast offers conversation without pressure as well as a homely touch. Some bed & breakfasts are targeting the corporate end of this market quite successfully, appealing to the safety angle and the gregarious nature of women. Remember, if you are going to try for this market it can be difficult to access from the suburbs. An inner-city location, close to good restaurants, attractions and transport, would be a viable option.

Alternative lifestyles

The so-called 'pink dollar' or 'pink pound' is often talked about as a lucrative market and, of course, some bed & breakfasts are run by gay couples. Word of mouth works very strongly here. You could alert potential visitors by advertising in the gay press. The internet is also another powerful tool for this market. Your customers are usually tech-savvy so use their smartphones to book their short breaks. This market is not for everyone, but if you're comfortable with it, and it must be said that *if you are going to run a bed & breakfast you will need to be open-minded*, you will have a loyal customer base here.

People with a disability

This group, like any other, both likes to travel for pleasure and needs to travel with work. Remember that only a small percentage of people who come under this heading use a wheelchair. They do, however, often have *specific requirements*. If you are purpose-building a bed & breakfast you might like to consider this group. You will have some statutory requirements to adhere to, so we suggest strongly that you obtain a copy of the appropriate Act from your local authority or download it free of charge.

Again, this is a very loyal group, with great word-of-mouth potential. If you can cater to their needs they will frequent your B&B. You will find that many of the modifications you make for the disabled are also good for the elderly.

Dietary requirements

Some bed & breakfasts have had success with guests with particular dietary requirements: vegan, gluten-free, vegetarian and kosher. We would suggest you only try to cater for these groups if you share their predilections, as they want meals that are tasty. Usually, only someone who understands their needs has the ability to cater for these groups.

Family market

There is a growing need for bed & breakfasts to cater specifically for the family market with the development of well-designed suites that can serve as multipurpose, family and group accommodation, and can also revert to separate accommodation. The biggest opportunities are for those who are located in an area where there is a lot for children to do: swim, fish, ride horses, walk, visit historic sites and major attractions, etc.

Self-contained cottages, where the host provides a breakfast, often in the form of a basket meal, are becoming a very popular choice for families. At the moment, most bed & breakfasts are giving this market to caravan parks, which are refurbishing and building cabins at a rapid rate. B&B operators who cater for this market should do well, given that it is generally accepted as being affordable.

You will need to contact your relevant local authority before considering self-catering accommodation.

Another popular place to cater for families is a bed & breakfast on a farm. If you go down this road you need to create almost a storybook farm on your property, with sheep, cats, dogs, pigs and chickens that children can feed, ponies they can ride and a cow or a goat they can hand-milk. All this with appropriate adult supervision, of course! For the city child this would represent the adventure of a lifetime. Please be sure to talk to your insurance provider if you plan to offer activities such as these.

Some authorities will require specific zoning before you will be allowed to go ahead. Again, we suggest that you obtain a copy of your relevant local government and housing requirements to see whether your property is suitably classified.

Dos and don'ts

In this age of litigation, we wanted to explore how the bed & breakfast operator is affected by advertising 'No smoking', 'No children' and 'No pets'. We contacted various government departments to try and ascertain how the bed & breakfast operator was placed in relation to these exclusions and to anti-discrimination laws.

We found that, in this area, government departments tend to be reactive, rather than proactive. In other words, they will wait until a member of the public makes a complaint about any restriction before making a judgement.

There are many strategies you can adopt in order to handle difficult situations should they arise.

No pets

There are hygiene and health, not to mention safety, reasons why you should not allow pets in your B&B unless you have suitable accommodation for them. If you have your own pets you will need to advertise this to potential guests. There may be valid reasons why guests prefer to stay where there are no pets.

For example, they may be allergic to them. Have at hand the name of local kennels that house cats and dogs so that you can recommend them to potential guests.

TIP
Make sure your beloved pet is acceptable to guests before they encounter it.

Some B&Bs however, are successfully targeting this market and acting as hosts for animals. You would need to map out your intentions clearly to your local authority to ensure that you have all areas covered before you advertise the fact. You should also advise your insurers that you are catering for animals as it may have an effect on your annual premium.

No smoking

We believe that this is a valid 'don't'. Smoke gets into fabrics and furnishings and is impossible to remove completely before new guests arrive. However, we would suggest that you provide a sheltered area outside where your guests can smoke. Provide an ashtray (which you clean at least twice daily) and a small rubbish bin. This will stop butts littering your garden. When advising potential guests about your property, inform them of your policy, but let them know of this area outside. Be mindful that the laws relating to smoking change from time to time.

In most countries, there is an Act relating to health and safety at work that requires employers to ensure, as far as is reasonably practicable, the health, safety and welfare of all their staff when at work. This could include taking steps to protect workers from illness caused by passive smoking. Where rest facilities are provided for staff, a smoke-free area must be available for non-smokers.

No children

This is the tricky one. The anti-discrimination Acts (see below) usually prohibit discrimination on account of age. Blankly saying 'No children allowed' or 'Children not welcome' could be seen as discriminating against an age group.

You may choose only to cater for families with children at certain times, for example school holidays.

If you don't wish children to stay it is better to say: 'We don't have the facilities to cater for children.' If you do want to welcome children this could be developed as an interesting and lucrative niche market. But remember children will behave like children and you need to be prepared for what that may mean.

Anti-discrimination laws and the B&B host

Over the last few years there has been an increase in discussion about the rights of smokers, children and the disabled. In a society that is becoming more litigious, B&B operators need to know their position in light of new developments in anti-discrimination. Do bed & breakfast operators have special rights in light of the fact that they live on the premises and their business is also their home?

In researching this we came up with the following items of interest:

Question: *Is there a law that would prohibit B&B operators from having a 'no children as guests' policy? For example, they may not have adequate facilities to cater for young children.*

Answer: Most governments have policies relating to parental status and age, which state that no one in business can discriminate on age. If your B&B preference were not to have minors as guests, then to say that you don't have facilities for children might not be enough to stop a prospective guest from lodging a discrimination complaint against you. You can, however, apply for an exemption to this type of ruling. Your argument would need to be very well thought through and soundly based to have any chance of succeeding. One could consider saying, 'Our property is not suitable for children as there are no facilities to keep them entertained.' In this way, you have warned the reader in your advertisement that the children might not have enough to keep them occupied. Most parents on reading comments like that would select another property.

Question: *Does the law require a B&B operator to provide wheelchair access?*
Answer: Wheelchair access is not usually mandatory as some dwellings are not suitable for this type of access by their very nature but, again, there are no grounds simply to discriminate against someone who uses a wheelchair and wishes to stay at your B&B.

Question: *Can a B&B operator enforce a 'no-smoking' policy?*
Answer: You can specify no smoking on your property by placing 'Thank you for not smoking' signs in appropriate areas. There is unlikely to be a law that states that you *can't* specify no smoking, although this, as with many areas of the anti-discrimination Acts, needs to be tested in the courts.

Question: 🏠 *Is it reasonable for a B&B operator to take the following view: 'Because my B&B is the place where I live, I can set policy and make rules that would not be possible if the property was a large hotel or guesthouse?'*
Answer: Not really, if it means that discrimination factors are ignored and a law is broken. Common sense should prevail when dealing with these issues because litigation is both lengthy and costly. By couching your words carefully when advertising the features pertaining to your B&B, readers will be able to decide whether your bed & breakfast property is suitable for their situation. In considering this point, remember that people do not appreciate being misled.

It is important that you keep abreast of anti-discrimination policy in your own country or area, and subscribe to publications that can enlighten you on the issues that concern you and your bed & breakfast.

> **TIP**
> As you collect information on your area, including brochures, books and the like, keep them for later use. Guests will appreciate reading books on the history of your area, great walks, local attractions, etc.

4 Preparing Your Property

The first decision you need to make when entering the short-break holiday market is whether you are going to be a 'traditional' bed & breakfast with a few rooms and a cosy atmosphere. Or will you be a guesthouse or a small hotel, where there is more separation between you and your guests? The difference is governed by statutory requirements in some places and only you can make the decision as to how you wish to operate.

The main reason people choose the traditional bed & breakfast option is because the house they currently own has sufficient space to accommodate both themselves and potential guests. There are benefits: your guests have easy access to you, it is easier to keep an eye on your property and it is not as far to go to work. The negatives are that having a family life can be constrained by your guests, so you need to be conscious that guests can access your personal space, and it is hard to ever escape from work.

What is the best option? The main thing you need to consider is privacy. No matter which route you choose – or, due to property or financial constraints, have chosen for you – you need to ensure you and your family have some personal space where guests are unable to intrude. This is a statutory requirement throughout Ireland.

Your family area would include a bathroom, bedrooms and preferably a separate lounge or family room. Without this space the strain on your personal relationships may be too much to bear. It is also good for your guests, as they are less likely to feel they are intruding on another's life. This space is particularly important if you have children or grandchildren living with you.

Location

Position, position! For many reasons, this could be the single most important part of establishing a successful bed & breakfast.

The position of your bed & breakfast in relation to your market really could make the difference as to whether your enterprise will succeed or fail. An important factor to remember is that guests often like to be within walking distance of food and drink.

In order to determine whether your property is in the right position, remember to consider both people on touring holidays as well as those who are having a short-break holiday, the latter often within a short drive time from their home. International guests tend to look for properties that are close to public transport facilities.

To be a roaring success, with good occupancy, you need to appeal to both markets. Ask yourself the following questions about your property or the one you are thinking of purchasing:

- *Is my property near a main road or in a country town with easy access?*
- *Is my property in a tourist area?* Factor into your profit and loss projections the seasonality of the area and the likelihood that your bookings may fluctuate.
- *Is my property within a large metropolitan city?* Be sure your property is aimed at an appropriate market if it is in a suburban area and that it is well signposted, as your guests will not want to spend all their time finding you (although GPS helps). It is best to be close to public transport, especially for those guests who are touring, and to popular attractions. If you are targeting the corporate market your guests will need good access to, and to be within easy travelling distance of, the business district.

Local government and your bed & breakfast

Before you march headlong into deciding where you are going to set up your B&B, or whether you are going to convert your current home, you need to establish a relationship with your local authority.

It is also important to know that the vast majority of national/state governments are currently developing white papers that will provide suggested compliance rules and regulations that local bodies can apply to all those who are involved in the home-hosting business. Currently, in most countries the regulations governing traditional bed & breakfast operators are both onerous and expensive. It is therefore hoped that the new rules applying to this form of accommodation will be more realistic in meeting the expectations of both the host and the tourist.

🏠🏠 Firstly, there is a raft of planning permission and building regulations that can apply to those offering serviced or self-catering accommodation. As an example, if you are considering structural changes to an existing dwelling or adding an extension, it is vital that you contact your local authority for their advice and/or permission.

Policies on granting planning permission do vary, for example, on car-parking facilities and guestroom numbers. Even if you feel that your home has the facilities set down by local authorities, 'change of use' planning permission may still be required. Another suggestion is to get a copy of the relevant authority's planning approval guide.

For those of you who are planning something a little more ambitious, you might want to hire a consultant to act on your behalf. At their worst, relevant authorities can require mountains of documentation and it can save a lot of heartache if you hire a professional.

If you want to make a complaint against the handling of your application, you should firstly contact the authority itself. If you are still dissatisfied, lodge a complaint with a higher authority. When there is conflict, it is best to be guided by your own legal advice or that of a private planning consultant.

To convert, buy or build?

You need to establish whether you are going to convert the home you already live in, buy a new place or custom build a property if you can find suitable land.

Each option has its merits – what you choose will depend on your personal circumstance. If you only want your bed & breakfast to give you pocket money, a supplement to an already healthy financial position, we would suggest you convert the property you already have. If you want your B&B to provide you with a little more financially, and if your house is not in a major city or a tourist area, you may need to consider either buying an existing property or custom building one.

> **TIP**
> Consider self-contained cottages if you have young children as you will maintain greater privacy and reduce the chance of burnout.

An exercise in financial viability

To test the viability of getting your house ready to be a bed & breakfast, the following can be used as a benchmark. Using your notebook, go into all the areas of your property that guests will encounter, taking notes as to what needs doing in each of these spaces. Be sure to look at these areas through the EYES OF A PAYING GUEST or ask someone else to do it for you. If you do this exercise through the eyes of the resident property owner, you will be in danger of deluding yourself. You are going into bed & breakfast to succeed. Therefore, you need to view the property as a potential guest. You want to charge as much as is required, without being excessive. In this way, the maximum occupancy that you can comfortably handle can be realised. You will not achieve these goals if your product is not right.

You need to look at the following in every room:

Ceiling
Is the ceiling flaking? Are there any damp patches? Does it need repainting?

Walls
Is the paintwork in good condition and painted a colour that adds to the ambience of a guest bedroom and the look of your B&B? Do you have cracks or any structural problems? Do you have to strip wallpaper or replace it?

Flooring
Is your carpet or flooring in good condition or does it need shampooing or polishing? If the floor is polished timber, then do you need to revarnish or stain?

General
How soundproof is your house? This is particularly important in bedrooms, as nothing is more off-putting, or uncomfortable, than being aware of other people's more intimate moments.

Do you have adequate ventilation? Do you have adequate lighting? Are there any structural problems?

Is there enough space to give every guest bedroom an en-suite or bathroom? If your room rate is going to be high, your guests' expectation would be to have their very own fully equipped guest bathroom, possibly even with a spa bath.

Do you have enough storage area or wardrobe space in each guest bedroom?

Do you have appropriate fire-safety measures in place? In most instances a regular, legal inspection is required.

Do you have adequate hot water?

Further in this chapter we discuss all the extras you will need to consider when converting your house into a bed & breakfast. Once you have decided what work you need to do, ascertain what work you can do yourself and where you will need a professional.

Obviously, the more you can do yourself the better off financially you will be. The things you need professionals for should be listed. You then need to get at least three quotes for everything. It is worth the time and the effort.

After you have done all these things, you need to compare the cost with a projection of what you think you can earn. How much is too much money? As a general rule, you should only spend what you think you can get back when selling your property as a house, not as a bed & breakfast.

Tips for buying an established B&B

You have done the research and realised that your home just won't adequately convert to a bed & breakfast. Plus, you have decided that you want to make this your sole livelihood. You have a bit of money in the bank and you believe the best thing to do is buy an established bed & breakfast. That way, you should have a good income from day one.

When looking to purchase an established bed & breakfast you need to consider the following:

- *Why is the business for sale?*
- *Is the area in which the bed & breakfast is located overpopulated with accommodation providers and therefore bookings are low?*
- *Are the owners experiencing B&B burnout?* (It happens!)
- *Do they have children who have reached teenage years and the lifestyle is just too difficult to juggle?*
- *Is there a motorway or other development to be built which will affect the area?*

The first and last reasons are what you really need to consider. The middle ones could mean you might have a viable property.

- *How old is the business and for how many years has it been profitable? Have they been making a profit for the last couple of years?*
- *How much business is currently booked for the next six months?* Ask to see the reservations diary.
- Ask to see the visitors' book. Guests don't lie. If the business is well loved you should see it from the book. It also helps you understand what the guests love about the place.
- *Is the success tied up in the current owners? The cooking? The nearby historical sights? The architecture of the house?*
- *What percentage of the bed & breakfast's business is made up of return customers? How much, therefore, am I paying for 'goodwill', that is, the intangible contribution of the current owners? Is it valid?*
- *Do the books look accurate? Do the assets outweigh the liabilities?* Get the opinion of your solicitor, bank manager, accountant or financial advisor.
- *Have all renovations been undertaken with council approval? Is the property zoned for bed & breakfast operation?*
- *Is it in the right location?* As with the purchase of any property, location is an important thing to consider. You cannot be in an area where the reasons to stay are too limited for the business to be viable.
- *Does the B&B have the right qualities?*
- *Is the current operator irretrievably connected to the success of the bed & breakfast? Are they award-winning chefs who bring foodies to the establishment? Will my relative lack of culinary expertise be the downfall of the bed & breakfast?*

Convert to what?

If you are to turn your current house into a B&B you will, undoubtedly, need to make some changes. Guests choose B&Bs for their homely atmosphere, but what they want is the picture-book version of home – not the reality.

They don't want the family fights, the untidiness, the washing, the laundry, the cooking or cleaning, or the discussions on what to watch on TV. They want the conveniences of a hotel, but with a home-cooked meal, pleasant discussion, and touches such as fresh flowers and homemade biscuits. They want a room filled with good books, a bathroom with complimentary bath salts and oils, and the smell of freshly baked scones and freshly ground coffee. And increasingly they want an en-suite or bathroom of their own.

When assessing the changes you will need to make to your property to cater for guests, you will need to start from the outside in.

Signage

The cheapest way you can get your B&B noticed is with a sign. It needs to be in the style of your B&B's architecture, your other promotional material (stationery, etc.) and your area. Use a professional sign writer – the sign will create a first impression and it needs to denote professionalism.

Before contracting a signwriter or graphic designer to work on your behalf, you will need to contact your local authority. There are usually regulations on signage placement, height and type and sometimes on colours, particularly if illuminated. It's cheaper to find out the restrictions before you become the proud owner of a sign you are unable to display.

> **TIP**
>
> You never get a second chance to make a first impression. First impressions count.

It's also a good idea to ensure the name and street number of your establishment are clear to read day or night. Nothing puts guests in a worse mood than being unable to find your establishment if your street name or house number is hidden behind a hedge or cannot be read on a dark, wet night.

First impressions count

The first glance your guests have of your B&B will be the impression they will take with them. It won't matter what they find on the inside of your establishment: that first look of your unkempt gardens and a dilapidated fence will stay with them throughout their whole stay. That is, if they bother to come in at all.

The truth is, first impressions count. What you can get away with in your own home you cannot get away with as a proprietor of a bed & breakfast. The outside appearance of your establishment helps to set the tone of your business.

Use the following checklist to help ensure that your first impression is a good one.

- Your lawn is mown regularly, the path to your front door is free from overgrown bushes and hedges, and your path is free from cracks and weeds.

- The rest of the garden is regularly attended, with no dead plants.
- If your house is made of bricks then be sure they are clean – repaint when necessary. When you do repaint, don't paint over a problem. It will recur. Cure the problem first, then paint.
- Your fence is in good condition. Your entrance is free from spiderwebs. Letterboxes, door handles and windows are clean and polished.
- Light bulbs are changed as soon as needed and the outside is well lit at night.
- Any steps or tiling are swept and cleaned regularly – and checked for slipperiness.
- 🏠🏠 Signage to car parking and reception is clearly visible.

As for your garden, you need it to be as attractive as you can make it. When planning your garden think about the time you can realistically afford to spend maintaining it and design it accordingly.

For the summer months, it is a good idea to have some garden furniture so your guests can enjoy the sunshine and have some outdoor privacy. The advantage of this is that it is a great place for you and your family to also enjoy the sunshine and some privacy.

Think about the addition of a water feature of some sort. Not only are they aesthetically pleasing, but the sound is very soothing – just what you need in a bed & breakfast. Not to mention the fact that it is very good feng shui. The Chinese believe that water is the symbol of money. A water feature will help attract more money into your home. (They say!)

> **TIP**
> The most important thing about your B&B is to have a spotlessly clean front doorstep. People always glance down at the front door and spotlessness here gives an impression of care and attention to detail.

Your entrance

Your entrance is the first thing your guests will see on arrival at your establishment. It is your chance to impress them from the word go. You want touches that will exude warmth and friendliness. Go for a huge bunch of fresh flowers, a feature wall in a bright colour or an original piece of artwork. If your hall is narrow it might be a good idea to add a large mirror to help convey a sense of spaciousness.

It is a good idea not to go overboard with furniture in an entrance as it can create an obstacle course when carrying luggage. An umbrella stand and a coat rack or cupboard are ideal additions. You don't want guests traipsing water throughout the house. They will be pleased with your thoughtfulness.

Flooring deserves special consideration in your porch and hallway. You want a surface that is easy to keep clean and is hard-wearing. Tiles need to be non-slip or, if you have floorboards, you must ensure any polish is not slippery. If you choose carpet you should investigate commercial carpet – it is more durable and easier to keep clean than domestic-grade carpets.

Heating or cooling is another consideration. If you are surrounded by snow you want your entry to feel like a warm cocoon. Likewise, if it happens to be hot and humid you want your guests' first impression to be one of coolness and freshness.

> **TIP**
>
> Leave a small blackboard near the bell at the front door so when a guest is about to ring they will see their own names. It gives the guest a warm welcome!

Living room

As we stated in the previous chapter, it is important, if at all possible, for both your sanity and your guests', to have some separate space, other than your respective bedrooms.

We would suggest that the best option would be a *lounge* or similar type of room. For some properties, it might be your old family room, conservatory or former children's playroom. This room will give your guests space and allow them to feel more at home. The fact that you will have a separate living room gives you a place to escape to that feels all yours, not the property of the general public.

Research indicates that guests don't mind sharing living-room areas with each other, providing they can identify where they can sit. For example, if you have a living area available for two guest bedrooms then rearrange your furniture so as you have two settings. You don't want people trapped in their bedroom. Guests generally don't mind if other guests share their space, or even if it is possible to overhear their conversation.

You need *entertainment facilities*, particularly music. An assortment of books is a great idea, covering all genres. Board games are essential – people love to challenge their friends to a game. *Television* is another thing you will need to consider. Many people go to bed & breakfasts to escape from television, but others find it relaxing. Our suggestion would be that if you are going to have televisions, place them in the guest bedrooms (preferably in a cupboard) or have a separate TV room. If, because of space limitations, you have to put a TV in the lounge room, don't arrange all your seating to face it and, preferably, hide it in a cupboard.

If appropriate, be sure to contact your local TV licensing authority, as extra TVs may not be covered by your home licence.

One of our concerns is that of 'amenity creep'. Some B&Bs are emulating the atmosphere found in motels from the lower end of the market. Don't do this, because people who choose to stay in bed & breakfasts do so for the homely comforts and to avoid the impersonal atmosphere of a hotel. For example, avoid a TV in a guest bedroom that swivels out from the wall.

People love to sit around an open fire, so if you have one, be sure to light it, particularly on dull or cold days. This would be a memorable feature of your lounge room and will be a source of good publicity for you. If you have it, flaunt it!

Likewise, if you have a view of the ocean or mountains, exploit it! These things are what guests go away for – the romantic ideal of home.

Dining room

As the name suggests, a vitally important part of a B&B is one meal – breakfast. This meal needs to be taken in a place that characterises the ambience of your establishment. As much care should be taken with the dining room as with the bedrooms.

In the United Kingdom and Ireland, B&Bs have taken many different approaches to dining. Many places follow the European tradition of one large table around which all guests sit.

This works very well for dinner, if you are planning to offer this as an option. People will occasionally bring their own wine and, over a few glasses, feel happy talking with strangers.

One large, communal table, however, can present some problems at breakfast. Some people are a little shy in the mornings and tend to keep to themselves. A number of establishments have found that they needed to introduce a breakfast area made up of a few tables of two and/or four settings, or a large and a small table. It is a statutory requirement in some areas to have a separate breakfast table for each guest bedroom.

As for style, you need to create a room that both looks good and is practical. Remember, you will be serving breakfast, so you want to be able to access all the seats. The table or tables can become a feature in the dining room, with an interesting centrepiece. Chairs should be comfortable. People on holidays won't want to rush eating so you want them to feel comfortable sitting for as long as they desire.

When buying furniture be aware of the upkeep. If your table is wood it will require work – you will need to protect it from moisture and heat.

When looking to replace furniture, you should consider new furnishings that meet higher fire-resistance standards; ask your local fire authority if in doubt.

You can get some great buys at places such as second-hand shops. You also have the option of buying from a manufacturer or supplier of commercial catering furniture. For chairs, particularly, this may provide the best option for a larger establishment, as they will be comfortable, practical and hardwearing.

Ensure your dining room has a sideboard or bench of some kind. It makes it much easier when clearing tables and serving meals. It also has the added advantage of holding your dinner sets and cutlery. The only word of caution would be not to clutter the top with too many decorative items – keep it simple. If you have too much on it you will find difficulty in using it.

The crockery you use can demonstrate to your guests the style of your B&B. Remember, it is the small things that your guests will describe to their friends. Your everyday dinner set, with its scratches, chips and cracks, will not do for paying guests. That doesn't mean we're suggesting you run out and buy Wedgwood or Royal Doulton, although for some of you that might be appropriate.

We would suggest *crockery* that is of commercial quality. Any patterns should be under a thick glaze and able to withstand dishwashers at high temperatures. Tapered edges are more prone to chipping, so if you or your partner are clumsy, we would suggest choosing crockery with a rolled edge. Enquire at a retail outlet if there is a piece of china that could be tested for durability. Ask if the retailer has a discarded piece of the china of the type you are interested in purchasing, in order to test the glazing, or enquire about guarantees for the durability of the surface. The glazing can be assessed by running a knife across a glazed surface and seeing if it marks.

If you see a flaw, keep looking. Do not scrimp on china by buying the cheapest and, whatever you do, don't buy end-of-line china. Pieces will chip and break and you need a set for which you can easily purchase replacements or additions as required. Remember, you want china that is ovenproof, particularly if you are planning to offer dinner, and any china with metal embossing, such as a gold rim, may not be suitable to be put in a microwave.

🏠🏠 Commercial sets might be a good option for the larger bed & breakfasts and guesthouses as your crockery may get quite a beating. This doesn't mean you still can't demonstrate personal style. Buy some beautiful serving plates and dishes. Use beautiful cutlery and glasses. Use the best linen napkins you can afford.

Choose a style of china and glassware and linen that reflect the style of your home, and which may be a feature of your region.

Your *glasses* should complement your china. In some cases, where a B&B does not have a liquor licence, guests may be able to bring alcohol, with your permission, whether you provide an evening meal or not. At the very least, you will need glasses for red and white wine, sherry, port, champagne, mixed drinks, and water, soft drink or cordial.

Cutlery needs special consideration for your bed & breakfast. Again, we would suggest easy care. Stainless steel is much easier to look after than silver, not least because you will be able to put it in the dishwasher. It will still stain and smear, however. To minimize this, a good tip is to use boiling hot water and vinegar and wipe it with a linen tea towel once a week after it has been cleaned in a dishwasher.

Ornate designs can look wonderful, but are more difficult to keep clean. Choose cutlery made in one piece as grease and bacteria have a tendency of getting caught between the blade and the handle. Plastic, bone and wooden handles are not always a good idea, as they will not withstand the dishwasher. As you can see, you need to balance style considerations with practical ones. Do you want to be cleaning that beautiful silver cutlery every day? Remember that you do want the table to look special when set, so choose wisely.

Kitchen

While the design and size of the kitchen will vary tremendously in bed & breakfasts, this is always a main cog in the machine. Your kitchen may be used for cooking only or may have an eat-in function, which, while unsuitable or unlawful for guests, will be great for your family's privacy.

The main thing you need to ensure is *cleanliness*. You are now serving food to the general public and you need to treat this with the seriousness it deserves. The last thing you want is to risk food poisoning. You will need to contact your local authority to see what restrictions will affect you in your kitchen, e.g. larger B&Bs must have a separate refrigerator for the guests' food. Increasingly, there is a legal requirement for those preparing food for the general public to obtain a recognised qualification. This will cover all aspects of food handling, storage and preparation. Your local environmental health officer will have all the details.

The larger your establishment, the more likely you will be affected by commercial laws of some kind or another.

Make sure that all of your electrical equipment is safe, as you have the responsibility to comply with the regulations set down. See your local authority about regulations and inspection requirements.

For health reasons, cutting boards should be labelled. For example, green for vegetables, red for meat, with matching colour-coded wiping cloths. Once again, it's a good idea to obtain a copy of the relevant health-and-safety legislation to be sure that your equipment complies with standards.

When it comes to design, you need to remember preparing meals for a number of guests will require significant workspace in the form of a large bench and or table.

At the minimum, you will want a dishwasher, a microwave and an extractor fan. You might also need to consider a bigger fridge and a pantry.

The other thing you must consider is safety. Kitchens need to be safe places in which to work. Kitchens and bathrooms are the most dangerous places in a home. Flooring needs special attention; for example, any tiles need to be the non-slip variety.

When it comes to kitchens, local government requirements tend to vary depending on the number of guestrooms applied for by the property owner. The best advice is to contact your local authority before making any drastic changes to your kitchen. Research has uncovered that legal kitchen requirements may change in the near future.

Your average residential B&B would require a double sink and dishwasher. High-quality detergent must be used due to the fact that the average dishwasher bought for the home does not heat to 77 °C (171 °F).

B&Bs that offer an evening meal will require all the above but the dishwasher might need to be semi-industrial.

B&Bs that have an attached dining room as a restaurant will need to comply with standard restaurant regulations.

Bathrooms and toilets

The days of expecting your guests to share the family bathroom are basically gone. That is not to say you can't be a B&B if you don't have separate bathrooms or en-suites for each guestroom. It means that you may not be able to have a room rate that is viable or an occupancy rate that is acceptable.

Another area to watch is the star-rating system that requires minimum standards, for example, bathrooms for guests only.

If you do elect to run with the family-bathroom proposition then be sure you have sufficient cabinets that hide the family's gear. If it's a grand and elegant B&B you have in mind, and the room rate reflects this, then the guest's expectation will be to access a fully equipped bathroom. This may include a spa-bath.

To en-suite, or not to en-suite, that is the question. If you can only afford to do one major thing to convert your family home into a bed & breakfast, installing en-suites is what you should spend your money on. More bookings are lost for not having en-suites than for any other reason, especially with international travellers. Guests will happily pay more for this option.

If you intend to accommodate people with disabilities then the bathroom and toilet facilities will need special consideration. You will need to consider safety rails, a hand-held showerhead and widened doorways. Again, floor tiles need to be non-slip. The relevant authorities will supply you with all the necessary details.

Given that you have heating in your bathroom, you will also need an extractor fan to eradicate all the condensation that occurs. Opening a window is not sufficient to maintain the controlled ventilation required to keep condensation and, in the long term, mould at bay in bathrooms. If you have sufficient room between your bathroom ceiling and the roof, the most efficient way to cover heating, ventilation and lighting is by installing a three-in-one heater, fan and light. For a little extra expenditure you will have a bathroom that is well lit, warm and well ventilated.

We would suggest that you replace shower curtains with doors, as there is less chance for errant water and thus accidents. Likewise, as another safety precaution, we would suggest that showers are not over your bath. This is another safety nightmare.

If you must use shower curtains, ensure that you wash them regularly. Nothing puts off a guest more than mould. Also ensure they are weighted at the bottom, so as not to wrap around your guests' legs when they are having a shower.

It is important to have efficient, easy-to-operate showers. Taps with a simple single action are the best ones. The flow of water from the showerhead also needs to be adequate. It is very hard to rinse long hair with a trickle of water! You need to ensure you have a copious supply of hot water. This is not an area where one can economise. Guests will always remember the B&B where they had a cold shower, bath or shave, and it will not be looked on favourably when telling their friends of their holiday break.

All your bathroom and toilet doors should be fitted with locks, and windows should be made of opaque glass or fitted with blinds. Your guests want to feel as if their stay is a retreat and not a peep show. The locks are particularly important if guests are sharing a bathroom.

You also may need to consider adding power points to large bathrooms. Special waterproof points are available and are a legal requirement. At the very least, you need sufficient power points for two appliances, a shaver and a hairdryer.

Ideally, the bathroom area is self-contained, with the washbasin in the bathroom. This gives a classier atmosphere to the room. A separate toilet with a washbasin is also a valuable facility if you have the room.

When it comes to furniture in your bathroom, it should be kept to a minimum. However, you might like to consider a chair or stool. Ensure it won't be affected adversely by the dampness.

With bathrooms and en-suites, it is the extras that will win you brownie points with your guests. We suggest that you consider providing the following:

- Two good-quality, generously sized towels per person, which you change daily. You also need to provide a hand towel and two face cloths.
- Mini soaps and hair products, preferably from a place like Body Shop or another aromatherapy retailer. You might even be lucky enough to find a local person who makes natural products. These will need to be changed after each guest. The provision of soap and hair-product dispensers is a good alternative.

- Complementary bath oils, shower caps, shampoos and conditioners. These are a real treat and everyone loves them.
- Make-up remover pads. This is a great idea, as it will prevent your guests from using your towels for this purpose.
- Plenty of thick, luxurious-feeling toilet paper. OK, so it's a hidden luxury. So many bed & breakfasts get this wrong. Don't scrimp and buy the cheap brand. Your guests will notice and will not be impressed. Ensure your spare rolls are in an easy-to-find place.
- Candles, and some matches! These are particularly recommended if you have a spa. Nothing is more relaxing or romantic than candlelight, and isn't romance one of the main reasons your guests have chosen the bed & breakfast experience?
- Fresh flowers, preferably from your garden, or a small plant will brighten up the room and reinforce the impression that you are the nurturing type. Be aware that some guests may be allergic to fresh flowers, so you may want to advise them beforehand or be prepared to remove them.
- A hair dryer: forgetful guests will love you for this.
- A wastepaper bin with a lid: the more bins you provide the less mess you will need to tidy up later.

Bedrooms

If you are going after the luxury romantic-getaway market, you might consider having spa baths for each guest bedroom. At the high end of the market, they are a definite draw card. You can, of course, get a higher room rate for the privilege.

In some jurisdictions, there are now minimum bedroom size and spaciousness requirements that are as follows:

- Single rooms: 5.6 sqm/60 sq. ft
- Double rooms: 8.4 sqm/90 sq. ft
- Twin rooms: 10.2 sqm/110 sq. ft

Now to the 'bed' part of your B&B: the place where your guests will spend at least one-third of their stay with you.

The first point-of-call is the beds. This is the most important investment in furniture you will make – and you really must consider buying new ones. It is your guests' opinion of the quality of your bed for which you will be recommended most.

One of the most common questions we get asked is what should you look for when purchasing a bed. Firstly – buy wholesale. As soon as you register your business you will gain allowances with a wide range of wholesalers, from bed linen and bed manufacturers to hospitality suppliers. Take advantage of these and shop around.

We suggest you buy contract quality. These beds have the added advantage of being built for multiple and varied sleepers – so they will last you longer in the long run. Most importantly, they are reinforced around the sides – the first place your guests will sit when entering their guestroom.

If you have a number of guestrooms, purchase queen-size beds – doubles are too small for most couples – and have at least one room with two single beds that will zip up into a queen- or king-size bed. With more and more friends travelling together, along with mothers and daughters and colleagues, the ability to offer twin beds will give your potential guests another reason to stay with you.

In general, the star-rating system calls for minimum bed sizes, for example, a single bed must not be smaller than 190 x 90 cm/6 ft 3 in x 4 ft and a double bed 190 x 137 cm/6 ft 3 in x 4 ft 6 in. Beds of 183 x 75 cm/6 ft x 2 ft 6 in will only be acceptable for children in a family-room situation. Beds of 190 x 122 cm/6 ft 3 in x 4 ft are acceptable for single occupancy only.

Bunk beds that cannot be used by adults must have a 75 cm/2 ft 6 in clear space between the mattress of the bottom bed and the underside of the top bed.

Note: It's advisable to download the star-rating programme from your preferred tourism authority in order to be sure that you have met all minimum requirements.

As for brands, we recommend Sealy. Why? They understand the needs of the hospitality industry, including B&Bs. The coverings all meet the UK furniture industry's stringent regulations. The single zip-up model has the option of an all-over covering. All their commercial beds are Health Shield protected, which protects against the build-up of mould, mildew, bacteria and dust mites. The coverings are fire retardant. Sealy also provide a service that will show you how to care for the bed longer term. Their contract division, which will deal directly with you, can provide you with substantial savings.

A rack or suitable place for luggage in the guest bedroom is important. This prevents suitcases ending up on the bed, bringing with them dust or dirt from outside.

You will need to supply electric blankets during the colder months. You need two pillows per person. You need at least two sets of bed linen per bed – more if you don't want to wash every day.

Think seriously about domestic linen if you are a larger bed & breakfast. It will need to be able to withstand the daily washes and coloureds will fade very quickly.

Normal household bedsheets have an average life expectancy of three hundred washes as against those used in hospitality able to last for five hundred washes – they tend to be 50 per cent polyester and 50 per cent cotton. There are a number of linen suppliers to the hospitality industry. Look them up in the telephone directory or online. Ensure that you have spares of everything (blankets, pillows, sheets) in a cupboard in the guestroom in case the guest's preference is for something different from the bedding provided.

> **TIP**
> Leave extra pillows and towels in each guest bedroom.

It is important to have a sheet and a light blanket as an alternative to a continental quilt. Many guests find even light quilts too hot.

When it comes to décor it needs to be neither too feminine nor too masculine. What it cannot be is childlike. You hear 'horror' stories from guests who have gone to a bed & breakfast only to find themselves sleeping with pictures of fairies, and 'Milla's Room' on the door. Guests want to feel that the room they are staying in is theirs for the duration, so unless their name is Milla and they are eight years old, this room won't achieve it for them.

Floors should be carpeted or have rugs to help absorb noise and keep the room warmer in winter. It is very important that your window coverings, whether they are curtains or blinds, give total darkness in daylight. Your guests will probably want to sleep in and you need to ensure they can do so with ease.

You need bedside lights on both sides of the bed and plenty of accessible power points to cater for everything people travel with. Don't hide power points under the bed or behind furniture! What you don't want is double adaptors – they are extremely dangerous (see Chapter 9). All guest bedrooms should have a source of heating, with clear directions if needed.

Guest bedrooms must have locks on their doors. If your guests are staying for more than one night then they will want to keep personal effects in their room. They may feel they can't if there is no lock on the door and other guests can access their space.

As for furniture, the most important piece, other than a bed, is a wardrobe – for those of you without fitted wardrobes.

TIP
Some B&Bs have a small table and chairs for two in the guest bedrooms.

You should supply at least five good-quality hangers per guest, and definitely not the bent-wire variety!

Bedside tables are important, with a tallboy or shelves for folded items. We would recommend a chair, and a desk is often appreciated – pens and notepaper are a nice addition. Don't forget the wastepaper basket in every room. An adequate mirror is also essential!

🏠 When it comes to extras – think of everything you would like in the perfect bedroom and try to provide it. A jug and glasses are always appreciated. Mints are good. Tissues are essential.

TIP
A chocolate on your guest's pillows is a nice touch.

Candles are a great idea – a great way to help create a romantic mood. Mini CD players are also appreciated. If you want to go all out you could provide guest robes, a must when guests have to go out of their room to access the bathroom.

Some people also appreciate facilities to make their own coffee and tea in their room.

Home Office

It is a good idea to set up a home office. You will need a space where you can do your paperwork, and set up your computer, a printer and any other equipment you might need. The tax system requires you to keep precise records of your business activities and it is a great idea to have a dedicated room in which to do this.

TIP
Have a list of items that are available for guests who may have left things at home, for example, toothbrush, toothpaste, nail file, comb, aspirin, etc. For purchase, if necessary, or to just give them on request.

Your accountant/financial consultant will be able to advise whether there is a tax benefit here – there very likely will be.

How and where you set this up is a personal choice. Our main suggestion would be that you do not put this equipment in your bedroom. Your B&B will invade much of your personal space and you need one room in your house that is exempt from work.

Building and development applications

Before authorities adopt a code or policy, it usually goes through a process of community exposure and consultation. The trouble here is that most people show little interest in these things until their proposed plan is directly affected. It's always better to obtain all the information and satisfy requirements from the outset.

Approval has traditionally been granted to operate a home occupation (yourself) or a home industry (where you might employ other people). In granting this approval authorities would again consider local amenity issues. For example, would it be noisy, have a lot of traffic coming and going, or incur other nuisance and environmental issues. Of course, there are some informal, unapproved operations in existence, which authorities might not actively pursue, unless they get a complaint about them.

Approval and construction of B&B accommodation

The most daunting part of starting a B&B might be dealing with your local authority. It sounds pretty simple to set aside a couple of bedrooms, advertise in the local paper, set up a website and in roll the customers. But don't forget that you will probably need the approval of the local authorities before you start operations or, before you know it, an officer will be knocking on your door and asking for an explanation.

Dealing with your local authority can either be like talking with a close friend or your worst nightmare realised. A combination of official zeal and ignorance can make the whole process confusing and frustrating. Suddenly the seemingly simple can become very complicated.

Usually, you will need to obtain *planning approval* for the use of the premises as a B&B plus building approval if any structural alterations or other modifications to the building are necessary. The good news is that usually you can make a combined application for both planning and building approval, which should speed up the process. In some instances, the approvals, and certainly the building component, can be obtained through a private certifier.

A lot of the codes and policies are now written in a performance format, which means that authorities give you a series of objectives and some suggested ways of meeting those objectives. You have the flexibility to decide what you will do to achieve the requirements. However, you may still encounter some prescriptive requirements – which simply state what you must do. While this format removes any doubts about getting it right, it also takes away some of the opportunity for flexibility and innovation.

Sometimes, you will be hard pressed persuading authorities of the merits of your vision for your individual establishment, particularly if it deviates in some way from the rules that have been set down. Appeal rights against an authority's decision may vary and become so costly and time-consuming as to make your proposal unviable.

It would be much better to negotiate as much as possible in the initial stages.

The thing to be aware of is that different parts of a building can have different classifications depending on the use of the individual parts. This can have important implications for the final classification of a building and the required type of construction.

Note: The impact that the short-let Airbnb reservation programme has had on the home-hosting industry means that national and state governments have developed or are developing white papers that will affect the way in which this form of accommodation behaves.

These white papers will ultimately come out with a set of regulations that property owners will need to abide by if they want to continue in this business. There will be two sets of regulations, one for traditional B&Bs and one for the short-let market.

Regulations for the short-let market may dictate the number of nights you can trade, possibly even introducing a licence fee, and, in the case of apartment owners, might allow authorities to charge the property owner an amount that covers the cost of additional rubbish-bin collection, for instance.

The regulations hopefully won't be so onerous as the ones in the past for the more traditional B&B/guesthouse/farmstay operation.

Fire safety

Fire-safety guides will tell you what you have to do to comply with fire-safety law, and will help you find out how to conduct a fire-risk assessment and identify the general fire precautions you need to have in place.

At the very least, you would be required to install a system of hard-wired *smoke alarms* in every guest bedroom and in hallways linking guest bedrooms.

If there is no hallway, smoke alarms would need to be installed in areas between guest bedrooms and the remainder of the building, and between each storey. The smoke alarms in hallways and areas outside guest bedrooms will also be required to incorporate a light to be activated by the smoke alarm, or alternatively the smoke alarms can be wired to activate existing hallway lighting to assist evacuation of the occupants in the event of a fire.

In essence, the building must strictly adhere to all fire regulations and have fire doors, fire extinguishers, smoke alarms and fire points. Where possible, bedroom windows must be all designed to act as emergency exits. It's also a good idea to have the fire alarm connected directly to the local fire station.

Fire blankets should be of a size to meet the expected risk. Your local fire brigade, fire authority or specialist fire-fighting supply and installation companies should guide you in your selection and installation of both fire extinguishers and fire blankets.

If you are required to provide fire-safety measures and facilities, such as smoke alarms, evacuation lighting, portable fire extinguishers and fire blankets, there will be regular inspections to verify that these measures are in place, are maintained and are capable of operation at an acceptable standard that will afford occupants of the building the required level of fire safety. The fire authority requires that fire-safety measures are inspected by an appropriately qualified person who can certify that the measures are capable of working properly – and these inspections are certainly in your own interest as they limit liability.

Depending on the nature, extent and location of any additions or alterations that you might want to carry out on your building, the authority may also require you to upgrade the fire protection between your building, any associated structures on your land and adjoining properties. This will depend on the existing and proposed separation between the buildings and property boundaries.

Of necessity, this information is of a general nature only and may not be directly applicable to your circumstances, in which case individuals should seek expert advice. Would-be bed & breakfast owners will need to check the new legislation and its application at the time of any proposed development.

Existing B&Bs will be expected to comply with the pending new legislation.

Advice for the home renovator

The basic structure of your property will determine whether it is viable to renovate or not. If the house has deteriorated in the worst sense then you could be faced with rebuilding the house from the ground up and the cost of doing so is seldom reflected in the market value of the improved property.

If your house has already been renovated, unless your vision contains only minor changes, it can be very costly to undo someone else's work. It is often easier and less costly to start with a blank canvas.

Renovating requires almost a Zen-like philosophy – you require patience, adaptability and a good sense of humour to endure the ongoing chaos. Keep the dream alive, the inspiration flowing and the lines of communication wide open. And practise the art of compromise!

> **TIP**
>
> If the cost of renovating your property results in a market price over and above the reasonable value of similar properties in your area, then it probably isn't worthwhile.

When you are thinking of renovating

1. View your house as four walls and a roof, taking it back to the bare structure. Look at what you do have, and what you don't have. Look at ways to enhance what you have to achieve what you want, before taking to the house with a demolition tactic. It may save you a fortune in the long run. Be flexible with your ideas.

2. Look around your area for houses similar to that which you would like, taking note of market value. Will it be cheaper to build elsewhere or buy a cheaper property to renovate? Even if you are looking at a long-term investment, it is important to stay focused on market value.

3. Ask yourself what effect you are hoping to create: olde worlde, modern, rustic, oriental, practical or luxurious are just a few examples. Do your existing windows, ceiling heights and any other things that cannot be changed lend themselves to this particular idea?

4. Will the furniture that you need to buy to create the finished effect fit into the room? You would be surprised how many people have ordered furniture that will not go through their doorways!

5. You must be able to see the potential of the property. Some people are better at this than others, but there are ways to learn. There is no point

in listening to someone else convincing you of potential if you can't see it yourself.

6. Consult a professional before you purchase or before you make the decision to renovate. Speak to an architect or builder, or even someone you know as a seasoned renovator, to get an understanding of the achievable and possible, and what it will cost to arrive at your dream. Unless you have a sound understanding of housing structure, get a qualified building inspection done, and include this as a condition of purchase.

7. Balance your renovations between personal requirements and general market appeal. Over-specialising your property will narrow your resale market considerably.

8. Consider the layout of the house. It is much easier and cheaper to embellish the original layout of the house than to completely reinvent the entire house.

9. Remember the most expensive part of any renovation is the labour content. The more work you can do yourself, the cheaper your renovation will be.

10. 🏠 To be realistic, set yourself a time frame, and then double it. This applies to using contractors, and more so to the 'do-it-yourself' (DIY) renovator. A 'simple' job seldom is, and untold catastrophes can occur. Furthermore the constraints of full-time work, raising a family and social commitments can see your time allocated for renovating ebb and flow – so too your enthusiasm.

Be careful what building company you use. Always get more than one tradesperson to advise and quote you for the work required.

If the work you are having carried out is on a large scale then you should consult a surveyor. Remember, you may need planning permission for some renovations. However, if you have just moved into your home you should already have had a structural survey done.

Take into consideration that some renovations may require planning permission and may have to satisfy building regulations; for example, a new roof covering. The planning department in your locality will be able to advise you.

> **TIP**
>
> Before painting a complete room use a tester tin. Paint a patch on different walls, as each will reflect the colour differently.

Planning permission

How much you can extend the dwelling will depend on your local authority and their individual policy. It also depends on the property type you wish to alter. There can be different limits on bungalows, semi-detached, detached, end-of-terrace and terraced properties.

There is not always a need to gain planning permission as some extension work and loft conversions can be done under *permitted development*. This allows you to build a certain amount without submitting plans. Each government or local authority has a different, and definite, policy on what meterage is acceptable.

If you don't need to get planning permission, then in some cases a *certificate of lawful development* can be issued to you. It will show that you have submitted plans and that you were legally allowed to carry out the works.

If you are building a garage then planning permission is not always needed; once again, each authority has its own policy on meterage and siting.

The roof of the garage also needs to be taken into consideration, as there are different policies for pitched and flat roofs. Permitted development is not available on all properties, such as a listed building, a building near a conservation area or new housing developments. These will all have their own set of policies.

> **TIP**
>
> It is a good idea to occasionally spend the night in one of your guestrooms, testing the room's appeal, the condition of the bed and your bathroom facilities. This will help you gauge the service you are offering.

5 Doing Your Homework

Your planning

Over the past few years, speaking to hundreds of prospective bed & breakfast owners, we have often faced the dilemma of how to sound enthusiastic about people's prospective ventures, while still issuing a word of caution.

To many people, more than any other venture, owning and operating a bed & breakfast represents a romantic ideal. We see normally rational people – doctors, lawyers, business owners, teachers, police officers, process workers – about to take huge financial risks on a venture for which they have not written a feasibility study.

No matter what your financial or personal expectations for your new venture, it is a business and you need to treat it with the gravity it deserves. You will find it impossible to achieve the results you want without a blueprint on how you plan to get there.

In this chapter, we aim to give you some advice that you may find helpful to get you started in your venture.

If there was one piece of advice that we would give you it is: 'BE PREPARED.' More businesses fail due to lack of planning and ongoing financial management than for any other reason.

So why don't people plan to succeed? The main reason cited is time, or the lack of it. MAKE TIME. This is your life or livelihood we are talking about. A few extra months planning your venture and researching the business you are thinking of entering WILL make the difference between success and failure.

Get out the notebook we talked about in the first chapter and write down your answers to the following questions:

- Do you have any business experience? Write down how you believe you can use this experience in your business.
- Do you have any other experiences you can draw on? How do you believe they will help you?

- Have you spoken to an accountant, financial advisor or business consultant?
- Have you contacted your region's tourism office to get information on your area's tourism statistics? Ask them for the number of B&Bs in your area.
- Have you contacted your local authority to get their position on bed & breakfast?
- Have you spoken to at least five other operators about their bed & breakfast experience?
- Have you stayed in at least five bed & breakfasts? This is important so that you can test the adequacy of the bedroom and specifically the bed and the bathroom against your perceptions. Write down the things you believe these B&Bs are doing well, and the things you believe they could improve on. Ensure that your plan addresses these issues.
- Why do you believe there is a demand for another bed & breakfast in your area? What will be your main advantage over your competitors?
- Have you spoken to your area's bed & breakfast association, if there is one? Have you contacted the national office?
- Is your bed & breakfast to be a lifestyle change or a commercial venture in the standalone sense?
- Are you buying an existing business? Have you contacted your financial advisor or business advisor to help you assess the business? Have you had a building inspection?
- Have you determined the financial goals you have for the business?
- Have you discussed with your financial advisor or business consultant the effect that turning your house into a business will have on your financial affairs?
- Have you looked at various tourism and industry publications?
- Have you sought the opinions of potential customers and suppliers?
- Have you worked out how much it will cost you to turn your house into a bed & breakfast? Did you get three quotes for all work you are not going to do yourself?
- Have you worked out a financial plan to supplement your income while you build your business?

Financing

In the first year of your new enterprise, you should try and finance your venture yourself. However, if additional funding is necessary, you need to ensure you contact your small-business association or consultant, your bank or building society, or a financial advisor. Remember, all start-up businesses need initial seed capital and bed & breakfast is not an exception.

You need to take the answers of all the questions above to any meetings you have regarding finance. It will show you have done your preparation and will keep you focused.

Starting your own bed & breakfast

So why start your bed & breakfast from scratch rather than buy an existing business?

- Firstly, you are not paying for goodwill or that intangible stamp the current owners have put on the property. The value of the property is one thing; the individual character, if proven, is something else. Both aspects are treated separately.
- Any reputation an establishment has is the reputation it has earned. If selling or buying an existing bed & breakfast, remember that the B&B or guesthouse name, attached to the property, can be part of the sale or purchase or a point of negotiation.
- You don't need to spend a lot of money at once. Your capital outlay can be gradual.
- You avoid the exit and entry costs of selling and buying a property.
- You will have the satisfaction of building the business from an embryo to a living, breathing thing.

However, starting a bed & breakfast from scratch is not all beer and skittles.

- You will have all the set-up tasks associated with starting a bed & breakfast: finding good suppliers, buying beds, dealing with contractors, etc.
- You will need to work in conjunction with your tourist association to build a relationship.

- You will need to live off your savings or paying job until people hear of you.

Buying an established B&B

So, are we saying that buying an established bed & breakfast is better? No, just different. The advantages are as follows:

- There is no start-up period.
- If you are a good operator with a solid business you could have a substantial positive cash flow from the word go.
- A marketing strategy is already in place. Your business should already be listed in your area's tourism brochure and a nationally recognised B&B guide, so you have a place in two popular bed & breakfast guides for your region.
- If purchasing, your predecessors already have an identifiable target market. This does not mean you can't change it over time, but for now you have a ready and, hopefully, willing clientele.
- Most of the establishment decisions have been made – and as you have purchased the property we will take it for granted that you believe the decisions were the right ones. That leaves you to get on with the business of the day-to-day running of the establishment.

Are there disadvantages? Certainly.

- You will be investing a large amount of capital immediately. If this is to be your career then that is not such a problem; if just a way to earn some extra cash, then the financial commitment could be far too large.
- You could be paying far too much for your prospective business. You need to determine how important the previous owner was to the business, and how much return business you can expect when considering the purchase price. Look at the visitors' book and assess how much the business could potentially suffer during the changeover period.
- You will be tying up your funds in a business that takes time to sell, if the need arises. You will be paying more than if it were just a family home. Be aware of this before making any decisions.

- You need to assess whether what you are paying for the furniture, en-suites, china, etc. is a reasonable price.

A copy of the audited tax receipts for the last three years will be required to enable your accountant to better advise you on the viability of the business for sale and how much it is really worth.

If you choose to buy an existing B&B then remember that you are making two decisions:

1. A property decision.
2. A business decision.

You must know how much the vendor wants for the property as against how much they want for the business. If you follow this, you are on the way in making a better commercial decision.

Is it going to work?

In order to make sense of all the above, you need to first test the viability of your proposed B&B investment by completing a *feasibility study*.

It is important to remember, however, that knowledge is not an end in itself. You must use the knowledge gained from completing this feasibility study as your worksheet and stepping-stone to achieving your goals and aspirations.

The main message is that the research you need to do to make your bed & breakfast a success must be unique to you and your market. If the findings in your feasibility study are positive then the assumptions can be used as a basis for your business plan. It can also be used as a confidential worksheet for your own personal use and so propel you to the next level of commitment.

On the other hand, if the results of your study are negative, then move on.

Doing your homework

No matter how you view it, your bed & breakfast venture is a proposed business.

People go into business for many different reasons, e.g. independence, status, lifestyle, boredom or whatever.

The key and overriding reason for going into business is to make money.

If you don't make money you can't stay in business – it's as simple as that. All the other reasons quoted above are secondary.

It is well known that small businesses fail at an alarming rate, but what is not so well known is that most of these failures could have been avoided. There are two key reasons for failure:

1. The people themselves.
2. Poor management.

Many people are not suited to going into business. They may be deficient in people skills or lack the discipline necessary to run a business, or they are unable to cope with change, pressure, problem-solving, etc. They may also not be physically equipped for the demands of the business or, far more commonly, they do not have the back-up and support of their partners and/or family.

The discussion period
Once the idea has been formed, it is usual to have a discussion on the proposal and its implications. There is usually very little detail or information at this stage, and a high percentage of the ideas die due to an unwillingness or inability to proceed further.

The first assessment
The first assessment is a period where information is gathered on key facts such as location, costs, staff requirements, time constraints and a whole host of operating details. A lot of potential bed & breakfast operators lose their motivation or interest at this point as they begin to realise just how much investment is needed in the form of planning, time, money and effort.

The research period
At this stage, potential bed & breakfast operators need answers, i.e. facts and details upon which they can build a comprehensive picture of their proposed operation, the possible market, the methods of operation, etc. They need to undertake research to give them a realistic understanding of their proposed business.

Again, many more potential bed & breakfast operators drop out as their research shows their idea to be impractical, non-viable, too complicated or, very commonly, a resultant picture totally different from what was originally expected.

The appreciation of commitment

After conducting the initial research, there is a clearer picture of the commitment that has to be made with regard to time, money, assets and labour required to get the bed & breakfast up and running. Many people decide at this stage that starting a bed & breakfast is not what they really want to do.

Poor management

While approximately 50 per cent of small-business failure can be traced to people who were not suited to going into business, a further 40 per cent of failures can be directly traced to poor management, e.g. lack of planning, or poor planning, lack of finance (both start-up and working capital), incorrect management style, lack of experience and/or training, poor time management and, surprisingly, poor selection and use of professional support.

It is in this area of poor management that most failures can be easily avoided. Good management begins with good planning – and good planning must have accurate information upon which decisions can be made.

Issue analysis

We are constantly amazed at just how many people have the idea, sometime or other, of going into their own bed & breakfast business. On the surface, it looks a really attractive proposition, with plenty of positives and very few negatives. Closer examination, however, gives a different story. The number of people who have the original idea and then reject it is high.

This next section assumes that *you and your family* have already decided that you are suitable people to be in the bed & breakfast industry.

Your planning

The planning that you need to undertake at this stage of your thinking is not, surprisingly, what is commonly referred to as a business plan. You cannot have a business plan if you don't have a business!

What you should be considering is, *What planning must I do to put my business idea into practice?* You also need to evaluate the viability or otherwise of your proposed bed & breakfast.

You are, in reality, looking at putting together a feasibility study. The depth and direction of this feasibility study will depend upon the type of bed & breakfast you are proposing.

Are you looking at a standalone commercial venture or are you considering a lifestyle adjustment by using your existing dwelling?

Standalone commercial venture

It is deemed a commercial venture when you construct a building specifically designed as a B&B or acquire a property and convert it to a B&B. In this case, your study will look at your capital needs and potential returns from the following options:

1. to purchase land, construct and fit out the building and grounds, while providing yourself with enough working capital to survive the first three to six months;
2. to purchase an existing property and modify it to meet your plans and standards, while, once again, providing yourself with sufficient working capital for the first three to six months;
3. to convert your existing dwelling into a dedicated B&B operation.

In case 3, you are looking at investing your land and buildings (your dwelling) into the business and as such you must look at it as the equivalent of a cash injection. You will need capital to modify your property and you will also need working capital.

In all the above options, you are looking at starting a business in a highly competitive market and are assuming the risks that any business owner must face. You will need good management skills as well as capital to make your business succeed.

We suggest that you start by writing your own feasibility study. If you have to source finance for your proposal, the feasibility study is critical to provide your potential lenders with the information they need. If, however, you are fortunate enough to have sufficient capital available yourself, then the feasibility study will provide you with the viability evaluation and assurance that you will require before investing.

A lifestyle adjustment

This is when you decide to convert part of your existing dwelling into a B&B operation as a means of generating a secondary income. This may well become a source of primary income in the future.

This type of operation is quite common and our research has shown that the main groups to consider this path are:

- couples who are looking at taking advantage of an 'empty nest' as a result of their children leaving home;
- people who have lost their partner and want to stay active and have people around;
- retirees on fixed incomes, especially 'baby boomers';
- professionals who are looking at contingency plans for the future.

The common thread is that these people are looking at what may be described as 'topping up' income, that is, income to supplement other existing sources, rather than a standalone income as desired by the totally dedicated B&B group.

The feasibility model provided here is applicable to both groups, that is, for standalone commercial venture and the lifestyle-change projects.

The depth of detail you will need to provide for this study depends upon which group you fall into. If it is the lifestyle-adjustment group, some parts of the study model will be irrelevant and your financial analysis will also change slightly. The core elements, however, will be just as critical to both groups.

The direction of your feasibility study will be determined by your answers to three very direct and personal questions.

1. Do you have your family's support?
2. Are you prepared to adopt B&B as a way of life?
3. Do you know what you want in your personal life?

If you have a family, their support is essential to your success. Should your partner and family not be equally committed, then you could find yourself stretched, isolated and often times lacking critical support, be it in the form of back-up, access to family assets or even just someone with whom you can talk. Remember that you are asking your family to make sacrifices for the business and that you will be changing their way of life. Don't assume that they will support you – involve them and ask for their support.

> **TIP**
> A given: operating a bed & breakfast is not just a nine-to-five job.

When you think about it, it is easy to see that your role as host demands long hours. Uninterrupted weekends, as you may know them now, will disappear and the luxury of a private lifestyle will probably be non-existent, especially in the early stage.

To be successful, your life will revolve around the demands of the bed & breakfast operation and your guests. Are you prepared to accept this?

Finally, one of the greatest causes of stress in owning your own business is having a conflict between what you want to do in your private life and what you have to do in your business life. No business is worth a marriage break-up or serious health problems. Your business is the vehicle to provide you with the means of achieving what you want to do in your private life.

Therefore, it is important that you sit down and visualise exactly what you would like to achieve both personally and with your family. What private projects do you want to complete? What personal milestones do you want to achieve and how do you want to allocate your time?

We all have wish lists for such things as hobbies, holidays, acquisitions and investments, as well as prior commitments that we must keep.

It is only when these personal priorities are written down with a time frame for achievement that you will be able to foresee possible conflicts between your private life and your proposed business demands.

Writing your feasibility study

Someone once said that every dream must have the structure of a plan. The saying that you get what you plan for is very true. Your dream won't just happen. You need to develop a strategy to achieve that dream.

Creating a feasibility study for your dream is a practical starting point where you work through all the key areas you need to consider.

As we stated earlier, a feasibility study is an exercise to assist you in making your investment decisions. It is also a formalised analysis that can encourage meaningful discussions with your partners, family advisors and potential lenders.

When you write it, use your own language and your own writing style. To give your study some organisation, and to make it easier to write and read, adopt a structure for your layout and presentation.

Your study should contain the following sections, which you can adapt as you see fit.

Cover sheet

Contents list

1. Your business idea

2. Your professional support

3. Your target market

    3.1 Location

    3.2 Your premises

    3.3 Your real-estate decisions

    3.4 Operational issues

4. Your financial analysis

    4.1 Desired income

    4.2 Capital requirements

    4.3 Financial viability

    5. Your decision

Appendices

Let's now look at each of these items in more detail.

Your cover sheet is designed to identify your study and to display a confidentiality warning to prevent or deter any unauthorised reading.

Your contents page is simply an index of the contents of your study. It is an organisational tool to facilitate easy reading of your study.

Your business idea

This written outline of your business idea is designed to help you focus more clearly on what exactly you are planning in your B&B operation. How would you describe your idea to someone else? Why will your proposal be different from other B&B operations? Why should people want to stay with you? What will you offer them, apart from somewhere to stay? In short, why will your bed & breakfast operation be successful?

This one-page summary is not easy to write and don't be surprised if you rewrite it many times. However, the more clearly you express your bed & breakfast idea on paper, the easier it will be to achieve in practice.

Your professional support

The success of any business operation can be directly linked to accessing quality professional support. You will need key advisors and mentors to assist you in formulating your ideas, guiding your progress, and watching over you and giving you not only feedback but, most importantly, someone to talk to. Your professional team should comprise:

- your accountant or financial advisor;
- your solicitor;
- your banker;
- your insurance agent/broker;
- your B&B association representative;
- your business mentor or paid advisor;
- carefully selected tradespeople.

Your *accountant* should be one of your key advisors, not just someone who does your tax returns. You should consider using your accountant to guide you in such areas as:

- your preferred legal structure (sole trader, partnership, company, trust);
- your financial and funding options;
- your approach to your financial source;
- your books and control systems;
- your taxation requirements, registrations and returns including VAT returns where applicable, capital gains, etc.;
- your financial reporting and forecasts;
- your superannuation options.

We suggest you look around for an accountant that you can relate to: someone who can speak your language, answer your questions and, most importantly, someone not too busy to return your calls and give you help and advice *when* you need it.

Your *solicitor* should be used to check any contracts, especially leases, before you sign them. We are, whether we like it or not, living in an age of litigation and the best legal insurance you can arrange is to have a good solicitor. You should also use your solicitor to assist you when you construct your own legal checklist.

The *banking industry* is changing daily and it is unlikely that you will have access to a bank manager. You will probably be dealing with a lending or relationship officer who will be charged with looking after your account. Try and foster a relationship with your contact person but, before you reach this stage, have a good look around to see which bank is the best for you and your needs.

As far as *insurance* is concerned, remember that it is a highly competitive market (see Chapter 11). We suggest that you should look at obtaining at least three quotes before you sign up. We also suggest that you check with your local tourism authority and/or other B&B operators to obtain the names of the insurance companies they use and are prepared to recommend.

Your *B&B association/tourism authority* will provide you with the industry support, networking and back-up you will require if you want to succeed in the industry. Being a member gives access to market research, industry news, training, workshops and best practices by networking with others in the industry.

Having a good *business mentor or paid advisor* is only now being recognised as one of the keys to business success.

A business mentor is simply someone with knowledge and empathy who is available to act as a coach, a guide, a motivator and a sounding board. It is someone who can discuss your business and management ideas with you, and help you make informed and effective decisions.

Your mentor need not be someone totally specialising in the B&B industry. It should be, however, someone with business experience who can pass on advice, opinions and information to help make you a better manager.

6 Doing Your Feasibility Study

Your target market

Completing your feasibility study enables you to test the viability of your business proposition before committing large sums of money to a venture that may fail.

Remember that your bed & breakfast will not appeal to everybody and that you should be identifying the type of guests you want to attract, i.e. your preferred target market.

What type of guests would you like to attract to your B&B? The choice is yours – you should at this early stage make this decision. Would you prefer to be servicing the top of the market or the no-frills sector? Would you feel more comfortable with corporate clients or with family groups? Your choice of target market will be a vital factor in influencing your decision on where to locate and how to design your premises. If, on the other hand, you decide to use your existing dwelling with modifications, then you must determine what type of guest your bed & breakfast will attract.

The following table contains ten categories of target guests to help you to identify your prime market group and also your preference towards two subsidiary groups listed in order.

Socioeconomic considerations should apply in all categories, as should preferred age brackets.

TABLE 1: TARGET MARKET OPTIONS

Market Segment	Prime Market	Subsidiary Market 1	Subsidiary Market 2
The more affluent guests			
Couples			
Singles			
Families			

Corporate			
Guests with a disability			
Budget market			
Groups			
Gay/Lesbian			
Other, e.g. pets			

Note: Use one tick only in each column.

Having identified your preferred market groups, (this also indicates age and income), you can now look at your location.

Your location

When deciding where to establish your proposed bed & breakfast, we suggest that you and your family choose three regions that appeal to you and where you could all comfortably live. Be sure that they are within reasonable driving range from a metropolitan area (where the bulk of the population is) and/or on a major link road to somewhere.

These three selections are:

Region 1 ....

Region 2 ....

Region 3 ....

These three regions can now be researched for the following information.

Local government policy

In each of the three regions contact the local council town planning officer and ask for a rundown on all tourist-related development conducted in the region during the last five years. Find out what is planned for the future.

Another question to ask is, *What is the council's attitude towards fostering tourism in general and bed & breakfast in particular?* They may have a policy document on bed & breakfast operations that you could obtain, or the information may be available from their website.

Regional tourism

Visit each region's tourism office and ask them whether they think they are getting their share of the applicable state, region, territory or county tourist income. If not, then why not?

Ask them for a copy of their current tourism-growth figures and the projected ones as well. Also, find out the demographics of those tourists who visit the region and where they live. In all probability, you will find there is a predominant area. You need this information in order to determine whether your target market groups come into the area in reasonable numbers.

Find out how many bed & breakfasts are in the region, and what markets they target and are servicing. Most tourist offices have access to market research on travel patterns in each area and this information is available and surprisingly detailed.

Visit the region's Chamber of Commerce and ask where they think the region will be in economic terms in the foreseeable future.

It is also a good idea to visit some estate agents/real-estate offices to find out how the local property market is faring. This will give you an idea on property prices, availability and trends.

Your regional assessment

At this point we assume that you have personally visited all three regions and have the salient information to evaluate your findings by completing the following table.

TABLE 2: REGIONAL OPTIONS

Information Gained on:	Region 1	Region 2	Region 3
Past tourism development			
Future tourism development			
Attitude towards tourism			
Attitude towards B&B			
Policy on B&B			
Development attractions			
Ave. length of stay			
No. of tourists p.a.			

Note: Place either a P or N beside each item: P = Positive Result; N = Negative Result.

The information gathered when visiting the regional tourism offices, Chambers of Commerce, local government and real-estate agencies should now be marked in the table below, again by placing either a P or N beside each question in the applicable column.

TABLE 3: REGIONAL STATUS

Information Gained on:	Region1	Region 2	Region 3
Regional share of the tourist £/€/$			
Current tourism growth statistics			
Future tourism projections			
Visitor demographics			
Main point of visitor origin			
No. of B&Bs			
Predominant B&B markets			
Chamber of Commerce findings			
Real-estate values			

Having completed the above exercise you will probably find that *one* region in particular stands out from the rest.

Through this process of elimination, you have identified the region that is best for:

- tourism growth;
- sound and reasonable local government B&B policy;
- innovative tourist association activity;
- your target markets coming into the region in acceptable numbers; and
- real-estate values that are within your budget.

Let us now look at your proposed bed & breakfast premises.

In essence, you now have meaningful commercial knowledge about the region you have nominated in which to establish both your family and your B&B business.

Your B&B premises

Having meaningful commercial knowledge about your selected region, you can now set about planning the floor area of the dwelling that is going to house your family and your guests. Whatever your prime and subsidiary markets are, be sure that you plan the floor layout in such a way that it matches your guests' requirements. Remember, when people choose a bed & breakfast stay, they are often discerning guests. It is also vital to configure the dwelling so that the family's living requirements do not conflict with those of the guests or vice versa.

The following table will assist you when working out the facilities required for your guests.

TABLE 4: GUEST FACILITY OPTIONS

Guest Facilities	Yes/No	Number
Bedrooms with en-suites		
Bedrooms with access to fully equipped bathroom		
Private lounges		
Shared lounges		
Meeting room for corporate clients		
Family suites with bathroom		
Children's TV/games room		
Outdoor children's play area		
Car parking for guests		
Guest games room		
Tennis court		
Swimming pool/outdoor BBQ		
Dining room		

It is vital to know what your family requirements are and we therefore suggest that you complete the following table, which will assist you in itemising all the facilities required for your family.

TABLE 5: FAMILY FACILITY OPTIONS

Guest Facilities	Yes/No	Number
Bedrooms with en-suites		
Bedrooms with shared bathroom		
Drawing/Living rooms		
Semi-industrial kitchen		
Normal kitchen		
Pantry		
Garage		
Workshop		
Storage room		
Office		
Laundry		
Other (please specify)		

The information from these two tables should allow you to draw up a floor plan for your proposed B&B.

Your real-estate decisions

Once you have a floor plan drawn up, you can:

- Take it along to a carefully selected real-estate agent and ask them whether they know of any property for sale that has a floor area similar to the one you are seeking or enough space to mould to your design. Check also that the location of any such property is ideal for both the guests and the family.
- If you cannot find a suitable property to adjust and craft into what you want, then clearly you need to look for a block of land suitably positioned upon which you can purpose-build your bed & breakfast.

Whatever the outcome, you will need to visit your local council's planning department in order to be aware of their building code and to ascertain whether there are any impediments that could be costly to overcome or impossible to consider. When you visit the planning department, you will also be able to gain an estimate of their charges. These charges will relate to the lodging of your development application plus any other charges relating to your proposal.

Your start-up capital costs

Let us assume that you have followed our suggestions to date. That is:

- You have identified your prime target market; let's say 'the more affluent guests'.
- You have nominated your two subsidiary markets; let's say 'corporate' and 'singles'.
- You have identified and researched three regions, and selected one.
- You have drawn up a site plan that will suit your proposals and have checked this plan with the local government planning department.
- You have looked at your real-estate options and have found a property in the right location for you and your family and your guests, which can be adapted to your requirements.

Let us assume that this property has a value or purchase price of £/€/$400,000. The next stage is to work out just how much it will cost to put into place any alterations and improvements you want, together with the furnishings you require. We suggest you refer to your floor plan and construct a list of everything you can think of that you will require for your bed & breakfast.

The following table gives a hypothetical example of such a list, and enables you to identify the capital costs of purchasing items and improvements as required for bed & breakfast purposes.

TABLE 6: CAPITAL COST OPTIONS

Items	Y/N	Qty	£/€/$ Value
King-sized beds	N		0
Queen-sized beds	Y	4	4500
Bedside tables	Y	8	1200
Wardrobes	N		0
Carpets	Y	6	15,000
Curtains/blinds	Y	12	8000
Other bedroom fittings	Y	4	1000
Bathroom fixtures	N		0
Lounge furniture	Y	3	9000
Meeting room furniture	N		0
Electrical, e.g. TVs, CD players, DVD players	Y	5	5000
Dining tables/tableware	Y	4	4000
Office equipment	Y	N/A	5000
Tennis court/equipment	Y	1	20,000
Swimming pool/equipment	N		0
Outdoor furniture	Y	4	2000
Bedding/linen	Y	6	5500
Sundry/miscellaneous	Y	N/A	1500
Alterations to dwelling	Y		43,300
Total – £/€/$			**125,000**

Note: Y = yes, N = no and Qty = numbers.

The 'Sundry/miscellaneous' heading is for all the small and sundry items you will require, e.g. pot plants, umbrella stands, etc. In this example, the sundry item is around 1 per cent of your total furnishing and dwelling alteration costs.

The other major start-up costs to be considered are your professional fees, e.g. your solicitor and accountant/financial advisor, plus any stamp duty required on the transaction.

Your start-up capital costs can now be determined as per the hypothetical example we are now showing in the following table.

TABLE 7: START-UP AMOUNTS

Start-up Capital Costs	£/€/$
Purpose-built B&B or	Nil
Existing property purchase	400,000
Alterations/improvements	125,000
Local government charges	2000
Professional fees, i.e. legal, accountancy	8000
Stamp duty (if applicable)	6500
Total	**541,500**

Your financial viability

The easiest way to evaluate the financial viability of your proposed B&B is to focus on net profit. The reason for this is that you need net profit to pay for your living expenses and your loan repayments unless you have another source of income that will subsidise these payments.

In other words, whether your B&B is to be a standalone commercial venture or a lifestyle adjustment, you will need it to generate enough net profit to:

- allow you and your family to live;
- repay your loan principal;
- pay your associated taxes.

At this level of net profit, if all you can do is pay for these three outlays above, then you are, at best, just breaking even.

Net profit is usually found by the following rule:

Total trading income	£/€/$ _____
Less cost of production	£/€/$ _____
Equals Gross Profit	£/€/$ _____
Less all operational costs	£/€/$ _____
Equals Net Profit*	£/€/$ _____

* Before Tax and Drawings

Your feasibility study should adopt net profit as its main viability indicator.

This viability can be established in eight simple steps, as follows:

Step 1 Evaluate your personal net worth
Step 2 Determine your total funds/assets available for investment
Step 3 Calculate your total investment needs and your borrowing totals
Step 4 Calculate your real monthly living costs
Step 5 Estimate your annual net profit requirements
Step 6 Determine your required annual sales level
Step 7 Establish the reality of your sales target
Step 8 Make a decision

Let us look at each step in detail and in so doing, continue with the hypothetical example we were using earlier.

Step 1: Evaluate your personal net worth

Your personal net worth is simply a listing of all your family's assets and liabilities. This is a standard starting procedure for any investment analysis. In our hypothetical model, let us assume the following net worth.

TABLE 8: PERSONAL NET WORTH

Total value of all assets	£/€/$750,000
Total value of all liabilities	£/€/$150,000
NET WORTH (assets less liabilities)	**£/€/$600,000**

Suggestion: approach your own bank or financial institution and ask for a copy of their user-friendly worksheets. They all produce these to assist you with your net worth calculations.

Step 2: Determine your total funds/assets available for investment

From your list of assets in Step 1, determine which assets you are prepared to invest into your proposed venture, and total their value. Don't forget to include cash that may be available. These funds would also include any loans you may take out using property as security, e.g. a second mortgage.

In the example we are using, let us assume that your available equity funds are £/€/$58,500.

Step 3: Calculate your total investment needs and your borrowing totals
You will need funds for:

- your start-up capital costs;
- your working capital requirements.

Your start-up capital costs were discussed earlier (see Table 7), where we estimated that our start-up capital costs, in our example, were £/€/$541,500.

In our hypothetical example, we are assuming that the family home will be sold at a price that will enable purchase of the new B&B property, plus cover the payment of local government charges, professional fees and stamp duty. This means that we need to fund £/€/$125,000 for alterations and improvements.

Working capital is the amount you will require to run your bed & breakfast operation on a daily basis. You cannot assume that your B&B will produce income from day one, which means that you will need access to funds to pay for day-to-day operational expenses for the first three to six months. This may seem to be an excessive period, but you would be wise to check with your financial advisor on this issue.

The following table will help you determine your level of working capital.

TABLE 9: WORKING CAPITAL (£/€/$)

Item	Month 1	Month 2	Month 3	2nd Qtr	Total £/€/$
Operating expenses					
Accountancy					
Advertising					
Association fees – tourism, B&B					
Bank charges					
Gardening, e.g. pool					
Insurance					
Internet costs					
Laundry					
Postage					
Power					
Printing & stationery					
Repairs & maintenance					
Share of mortgage payments					
Telephone					
Travelling expenses					
Vehicle costs					
Wages & salaries					
Production costs					
Food & provisions					
Commissions on sales					
Cleaning					
Miscellaneous					
Total running costs	1400	1450	1500	4950	9300
Add non-perishable purchases	50	55	60	210	375
Total – £/€/$ value	**1450**	**1505**	**1560**	**5160**	**9675**

Note: we assume that you have put in your own costs in the empty columns above, but, in this example, we have assumed a total working capital requirement of £/€/$9675. With this information, it is now possible to estimate your borrowing needs. For example:

TABLE 10: BORROWING NEEDS

For assets needed, i.e. Table 6	£/€/$125,000
For working capital required	
(First 6 months)	£/€/$9675
Total funds needed	**£/€/$134,675**
Less equity funds available from Step 2	£/€/$58,500
TOTAL TO BE BORROWED	**£/€/$76,175**

Step 4: Calculate your real monthly living costs

We stressed early in this book that your business is the means by which you are able to meet your family's lifestyle requirements and budgets. Your own and your family's monthly living costs can be divided into three categories, i.e. fixed, variable and discretionary.

Fixed costs are just that. There is no flexibility in either their amount or their required date of payment, e.g. loan repayments, council rates, car registrations, etc. Variable costs can be adjusted in relation to their amount or their date of payment. Examples in this group are clothing, food, maintenance, etc. Discretionary costs are costs over which you have total control as to whether you want to incur them, e.g. gifts, entertainment, holidays, etc.

Living costs will vary from month to month, with some months being far more expensive than others. To get a realistic picture we suggest you look at your total year's activity and then work out an average monthly cost. For our assumed example, we are showing the following monthly living costs as:

TABLE 11: MONTHLY LIVING COSTS

Total fixed costs (e.g. rates, car tax, etc.)	£/€/$600
Total variable costs (e.g. food, petrol, etc.)	£/€/$1500
Total discretionary costs (e.g. holidays, total savings)	£/€/$500
TOTAL MONTHLY LIVING COSTS	**£/€/$2600**

Armed with this information we can now move on to the next step.

Step 5: Estimate your annual net profit requirements

The net profit you require must be enough to:

- pay for your personal drawings/wage equivalent;
- provide you with a reasonable return on your equity investment.

Your level of drawings must be sufficient to pay for your monthly living costs. In the example we are using, we have established our average monthly living costs to be £/€/$2600, that is, £/€/$31,200 per annum.

It is also standard practice to expect some return on the money you have invested in your bed & breakfast. (If you invested your funds into an external venture you would expect a return.) Let us assume for this example that a reasonable annual return is 8 per cent.

The profits you will need from your bed & breakfast will therefore, in this example, be:

1. Drawings of at least the level of your annual living costs (refer to Table 11), i.e. monthly costs of £/€/$2600 x 12 = £/€/$31,200 plus:
2. Return on invested equity (refer to Table 10), i.e. 8 per cent on £/€/$58,500 = £/€/$4680

   Total net profit needed £/€/$35,880

In the calculations so far, we have assumed your bed & breakfast to be a standalone commercial venture rather than a lifestyle adjustment. As a standalone commercial venture, the net profit figure of £/€/$35,880 is the minimum net profit you need just to break even. If, however, your bed & breakfast is not a standalone venture, and you have income from other sources, your net profit expectations could be much lower. If this is the case, we suggest you nominate the level of net profit you require to top up your other income sources.

Once you have established your net profit requirements, the next step is to look at the sales level required to provide you with this profit.

Step 6: Determine your required annual sales level

In our viability exercise so far, we have focused on net profit and worked out how much net profit we require to break even. Once we have this net profit figure, we can work backwards to estimate the sales level required to produce this net profit.

Working in percentages as well as cash does this. Let us look once again at the net profit formula, this time with the idea of expressing all items as a percentage of trading income.

TABLE 12: NET PROFIT ANALYSIS

	£/€/$	%
Total trading income	£/€/$	100%
Less cost of production	£/€/$	25%
Equals gross profit	£/€/$	75%
Less operating expenses	£/€/$	50%
Equals net profit (before tax and drawings)	£/€/$	25%

It is our experience that costs of production, e.g. food and provisions, can usually run at around 25 per cent of trading income.

Given this estimate, gross profit would represent 75 per cent of trading income. From this 75 per cent we have to deduct all operating expenses.

In a standalone commercial bed & breakfast enterprise, we believe that a minimum industry average of around 25 per cent total income is an acceptable level of net profit.

This percentage can be higher, contingent on occupancy levels, and whether you outsource tasks such as cleaning, etc. The more you do yourself, the higher the net profit. If your bed & breakfast is a standalone commercial operation, then we can assume in our example that:

1. the net profit needed is £/€/$35,880; and
2. this net profit is, say, 25 per cent of total income.

Our required sales or trading income required would therefore be: £/€/$35,880 x 100/25 or £/€/$143,520 per annum.

If, however, your bed & breakfast proposal is a lifestyle adjustment rather than a standalone business, you will need to look at the top-up income you require to augment your other income.

If this top-up income is, say, only £/€/$9000 per annum, then your sales or trading income required from your bed & breakfast will be: £/€/$9000 x 100/25 or £/€/$36,000 per annum.

Step 7: Establish the reality of your sales target

At this stage, ask the question: *Can guest bookings at this level be reached?* To gain a more realistic appreciation of your yearly trading targets, look at this as a monthly or weekly figure:

TABLE 13: CRITICAL AMOUNTS – SALES/TRADING TARGETS

Sales/Trading Targets	Standalone Business	Lifestyle Adjustment
Yearly sales target	£/€/$143,520	£/€/$36,000
Monthly sales target (12 mths/year)	£/€/$11,960	£/€/$3000
Weekly sales target (48 weeks/year)	£/€/$2990	£/€/$750

The answers obviously relate directly to:

1. the number of rooms available for guest use;
2. the room rates you will charge;
3. your potential and likely occupancy rates;
4. your marketing strategy and its effectiveness.

To help you work out your ability to meet your target income levels, we suggest you construct a daily room-rate income 'ready reckoner' similar to the following table:

TABLE 14: ROOM RATES PER NIGHT

Guestrooms	£/€/$ 120	£/€/$ 130	£/€/$ 140	£/€/$ 150	£/€/$ 170	£/€/$ 200
One	120	130	140	150	170	200
Two	240	260	280	300	340	400
Three	360	390	420	450	510	600
Four	480	520	560	600	680	800
Five	600	650	700	750	850	1000

This ready reckoner is a simple way of matching the room rates you select with the number of guestrooms available.

However, it does not take into account your expected occupancy rate. The next table allows you to quickly convert your guestroom availability and your expected occupancy rate into yearly anticipated bed nights. We are working on a forty-eight-week-per-year basis.

TABLE 15: OCCUPANCY – YEARLY BED NIGHTS

Guestrooms	15%	25%	35%	50%	60%
One	50	84	118	168	202
Two	100	168	236	336	404
Three	150	252	354	504	606
Four	200	336	470	672	808
Five	250	420	588	840	1008

By combining the information from these two tables you can:

1. nominate your room rate and thus set your daily guestroom income, for our example £/€/$170;
2. estimate your occupancy rates and thereby establish your anticipated yearly bed nights;
3. combine both to estimate your potential income. In the following tables, we do just this.

TABLE 16: STANDALONE COMMERCIAL VENTURE POTENTIAL GUESTROOM INCOME

Guestroom	15% £/€/$170	25% £/€/$170	35% £/€/$170	50% £/€/$170	60% £/€/$170
One	8500	14,280	20,060	28,560	34,340
Two	17,000	28,560	40,120	57,120	68,680
Three	25,500	42,840	60,180	85,680	103,020
Four	34,000	57,120	80,240	114,240	137,360
Five	42,500	71,400	100,300	142,800	171,700

Related to Table 13, the standalone commercial venture in our exercise would require five guestrooms at a room rate of £/€/$170 and an occupancy level of slightly more than 50 per cent to achieve the £/€/$143,520 yearly sales target needed.

The industry average occupancy rate for a well-run B&B establishment, located in an area where you can attract the corporate market midweek and the leisure market during the weekends, ranges from 40 per cent to 60 per cent.

TABLE 17: LIFESTYLE ADJUSTMENT POTENTIAL GUESTROOM INCOME

Guestroom	15% £/€/$140	25% £/€/$140	35% £/€/$140	50% £/€/$140	60% £/€/$140
One	7056	11,760	16,520	23,520	28,280
Two	14,000	23,520	33,040	47,040	56,560
Three	21,000	35,280	49,560	70.560	84,840
Four	28,000	47,040	66,080	94,080	113,120
Five	35,000	58,800	82,320	117,600	141,400

The lifestyle adjustment in our exercise above would require a minimum of three guestrooms, a room rate of £/€/$140 and an occupancy level of slightly less than 26 per cent. The average occupancy rate, based on mostly weekend trade, ranges from 20 per cent to 70 per cent depending on the season.

Step 8: Make a decision

You have now reached the stage where you can compare your potential income with the income you need if you are to match or exceed your break-even point that we calculated in Step 6.

If your potential income is below your break-even level, we suggest that you go back to your earlier work, re-evaluate your cost options, your expenditures, etc., and see the effect as you redo your calculations. You can ask the questions:

What would happen if ...

- *I achieved cost savings in materials, guest amenities, and so on?*
- *I modified the design?*
- *I was able to raise my room rates?*
- *I could increase my occupancy rate?*
- *I discounted midweek room rates?*

By asking these 'what if' type questions, you are, in effect, looking at possible modifications that could make your business idea more compatible with your personal needs and objectives.

Your decision

It is now the moment of truth!

Your feasibility study is, as we stated earlier, a simply formalised approach to assist you in making your investment decisions. It provides you with a facility to evaluate your options every step of the way. It will not, however, make the final decision for you. You alone can make that decision.

If your decision was simply a matter of evaluating the economic viability of your proposed B&B, then such a decision would be an easy one to make. However, there are other key factors which impact on your final decision to proceed. These non-economic factors are:

- your private/family lifestyle expectations;
- the willingness of your partner/family to match you in your commitment as a totally professional host;
- your understanding of the difference between a lifestyle adjustment and a standalone commercial venture.

After looking at the results of the viability of your proposal and also at the non-economic factors we have just mentioned, you may decide *not* to proceed with your bed & breakfast proposal. If this is the situation, then the feasibility study you have just completed has still been a worthwhile exercise. It is a lot easier to withdraw at this stage than it is once your venture is actually up and running.

If, however, you conclude that your venture *is* viable and that you want to proceed, then the knowledge gained from your feasibility study is invaluable and will form the basis for your business plan when you write one.

We repeat our earlier advice to you to make full use of your professional team when you are writing this study.

Finally, we wish you every success in your deliberations. Be reassured that you have taken the first step in a professional approach to getting into bed & breakfast.

> **TIP**
> Keep yourself up to date with short-break holiday trends. This market segment is about to take off.

Part Two

How to Run Your B&B Efficiently
and Successfully

7 Putting the People Back in Service

Service. It is a word that you will hear over and over again in this chapter. Being willing and able to provide exceptional customer service is one of the keys to being a successful bed & breakfast operator.

We spoke in the first part of the book about whether you were the right sort of person to be a bed & breakfast host. By now we can assume that your positives outweighed your negatives. Get your answers to the questions from Chapter 1 and read them again. Are your answers the same?

There is no doubt that having had some prior experience in a service industry will stand you in good stead when running a bed & breakfast. But if you have not had the advantage of this experience all is not lost. You have been a consumer your whole adult life. Take some time to think about the best service that you have ever received when on holiday. What made it so good? What about the worst service? What was bad about it?

Service is a strange entity. If is often about perception. To one customer your behaviour may seem cloying and intrusive; to the next, receiving exactly the same service, you might seem remote and cold. The level of service is the same, but your guest has perceived it differently. Often the perception of good service isn't about how guests feel about you at all. Freshly ground coffee first thing in the morning, the morning paper outside their bedroom door, freshly baked scones for afternoon tea – these are things that can make up good 'service' in your guests' minds.

> **TIP**
> Act and look professional at all times.

In this chapter, we are going to focus on how you can ensure that all the dealings you have with your guests are consistent and special for them.

Communicating with prospective guests
My name is . . .

🏠 Your name is an integral part of making your guests feel at home. All of your interactions with your guests, whether on the telephone, by email or in person, should be personal and nothing will get this across as quickly as you using your guest's name and their use of yours. Introduce yourself by your first name and ask your guest if they would mind if you used theirs. People stay at B&Bs because they like the feeling of intimacy and 'home' that they represent. Using your first name, and theirs, is an easy way to give your guests an identity, and make them feel part of your family – if even for a day.

Wi-fi/phone/fax

Ideally, you will want to invest in the installation of a wi-fi connection that allows guests to use their iPad or laptop. Having a phone/fax also allows other members of the household to make personal calls without fear of missing a booking. It is suggested that if you have young children you prevent them from answering this phone. If you are going out you can either divert your *business phone* to your mobile (another necessity) or put on your answering machine.

You will need an email account and/or printer. These are essential tools, given that you may wish to send your guest a sketch map showing how to find your B&B, among other things.

Answering the phone

Answer the phone with the name of your establishment and your name. Smile when speaking on the phone; a smile shines through and you can 'hear' it in your voice.

Always sound friendly, relaxed and courteous – you have already acknowledged you are a people person so this should be very easy.

You need to ensure that you have your *reservation diary* and a *pen* by the telephone. You don't want to have to ask your caller to wait while you get organised – it doesn't leave a good impression. It is a great idea to ask questions of your caller so you can determine things that may be of interest to them and build some rapport with them as soon as possible. Note the kind of language a guest uses, so that you can match the style when you are talking to them later. By matching your caller's voice tone you will make them feel comfortable with you. They will also give you much more useful information if they feel you empathise with them.

Most of all, you need to remember that much of your business will be won or lost by the information you present to your customer over the telephone or email and how you present it.

> **TIP**
> Learn to turn every enquiry into a booking, and smile!

Email

It is a very different world from even five years ago. Over the past five years, the internet – and the use of international reservation platforms – has exploded and the reality is that much of the communication you have with potential guests will be over the internet. Over more than 75 per cent of internet users who travel have used it to book accommodation over the last twelve months. This is a statistic that is destined to grow over time.

For potential international and corporate guests, the internet and email will be the main form of communication. It has the enormous advantage of being cheap and comprehensive, not to mention visual.

Ensure that the tone of your email is friendly yet professional. You need to check your emails regularly and follow up any enquiries promptly. Check your spelling and grammar as even something as minor as this can deter some potential guests. They may believe that if you care so little for your business that you did not take the time to run a spellcheck you might not care about the details of their stay.

Questions and answers

As much of your business will be won or lost by what you say over the phone or by email, there are a number of commonly asked questions to which you should have the answer, and there are some questions that you need to ask, too.

The following is a list of questions and subject areas with which you might like to start. As people ask other questions, write the answer down and put them with this list at the front of your reservation diary.

How can we reach you?

Even though many guests have a GPS device that will enable them to locate your property with pinpoint accuracy, you need to be able to provide detailed directions on how your guest might reach you by car, public transport or walking, particularly if you are down unnamed lanes or a little out of the way. You might also give those who don't have GPS some idea of travelling time and distance.

Ask that potential guest for their address or email so you can send them a map. Directions should assume your guests are arriving with a tired, hungry family on a dark, wet night. Your directions should be so good that they are able to find you without any assistance. If you have specific parking instructions – for example, some local authorities will not allow on-street parking – you will need to be able to provide this information as well.

They may even ask you to detail how close you are to local attractions with instructions as to how they might get there. Check-in and check-out times are also important.

Once your guest confirms the booking you will need to pinpoint their arrival time as closely as possible, so you can ensure you are prepared.

Reservation details

You need to be able to present room rates and feature details as a friendly salesperson would. This is your chance to win the guest's business.

Now is your opportunity to advise: how far ahead you need booking confirmation, of your availability, of any minimum-night restrictions (two nights on a weekend, for example), deposit details (how much, refundable or non-refundable) and cancellation penalties. You will also need to abide by the listing details procedures of international reservation platforms.

> **TIP**
> Offer to help plan a local itinerary; this can be done initially, in your welcoming letter or upon your guests' arrival.

At this initial stage, you will also need to advise how you accept payment – cash, cheque, credit cards, PayPal or through the reservation platform, e.g. through Airbnb, which pays direct into your bank account. Normally, the international reservation platforms allow you twenty-four hours to confirm that you can take their booking.

So what do you need to record?

In some countries guests are required to provide travel and personal details along with passport details.

Ask your bank for the application forms that would ultimately enable you to process credit and debit card payments, e.g. MasterCard/Visa. Many of your guests will expect this payment option. Obtaining a PayPal account is another option as many people use this financial gateway.

Features and benefits

You will often be asked by potential guests to provide information about the *features and benefits* of your establishment: the size of your rooms; any themed rooms you might have, e.g. decorated on a nationality theme; bed configuration; whether or not the room is serviced daily; whether the bathrooms are shared or if you have en-suites; if you have a spa bath in any of the rooms. This is your opportunity to promote your bed & breakfast. You need to be able to talk about the meals you provide and whether the guests eat with you or privately; you may even be asked to provide some sample menus.

You may be asked about alcohol – whether it can be bought nearby and whether there is a BYO (bring your own) policy.

Some guests, especially from abroad, may ask whether there are cooking facilities they can use such as a small kitchenette or BBQ in summer. Any extras you provide such as laundry facilities, irons, hairdryers, phone lines, internet access, etc., also need to be detailed here. If you have special packages for honeymoons, corporate clients, special school events or special interests, now is the time to offer to tell your potential guest about them.

Children, pets or smoking?

By now you will have determined your policy on these issues and you need to detail these to all prospective bookings. Better your guests know your stance now rather than having a possible confrontation when they arrive.

> **TIP**
>
> Always tell your guest at the time of booking that there is a no-smoking policy.

Special requirements

Guests may ask you whether you have *facilities for the disabled* and you will need to be able to advise on any modifications you have made. If you don't have appropriate facilities (such as wheelchair access) you need to advise the guest of this.

Dietary specialities are another thing for which you may be asked to cater. If providing a breakfast or evening meal you may wish to ask at the point of reservation whether any of the party have any food restrictions, e.g. gluten intolerance, lactose intolerance or vegetarianism, so you can plan in advance.

Local activities and attractions

You need to know *everything* about your area, as guests will have the expectation that you are their local guide to the city or region.

Sell the best parts of your locality to your potential guests as this could sway them in your direction and also lengthen the duration of their stay. You also need to be able to provide details of great places to eat in your area. Guests may ask you to send menus of local pubs and restaurants or even make bookings for them.

Written correspondence

A letter should follow up any telephone enquiries about your establishment, preferably the next day. This letter needs to be neatly presented and on a letterhead. As with email, correct spelling is paramount.

The letter should not give the impression of being a standard form, even if it is. Try to personalise the letter with some information that your caller asked for over the phone and use their first names, as well as yours.

If you are replying to particular questions, answer these questions specifically, not with 'our brochure is enclosed', although by all means enclose your brochure as well.

Once people have booked a room, follow up their booking with a written confirmation and a map. It is details like this that will make a difference.

Deposits and cancellations

Normally, one must honour the booking arrangement once the guest has accepted it. The only time it can be changed is when both parties agree.

Larger properties and booking agencies tend to have lengthy deposit and cancellation policies whereas smaller operators need only to have a simple set of procedures.

The deposit taken at the time the booking is made ranges from 20 to 50 per cent of the tariff, which may be influenced by seasonality considerations.

The cancellation policy, which should be put in writing, may represent the following formula:

Days prior to booking commencement	As a % of total booking amount
0–12 days	100
13–21 days	75
22–42 days	60
43–60 days	33
93 days or more	10

When to claim
You can claim the outstanding balance owing after the duration of the stay booked has elapsed.

Here at last
Now is the moment you have been waiting for – the moment you come face to face with your guests and welcome them to your bed & breakfast.

Again, you need to do your best to put your guests at ease immediately so they feel they are at their home away from home. Introduce yourself by your first name and, if you know your guest's first name, use it with permission, as it will help put everyone at ease.

Ideally, when the guests arrive and after they have freshened up, show them around and suggest that they come and join you for a quality drink and some freshly baked goodies. The morning/afternoon tea has multiple purposes:

- It will allow you to get to know one another.
- You can find out what they intend to do while staying in your area and it will allow you the opportunity to offer suggestions that will further enhance their stay.
- It will give you the opportunity to show off your baking skills. The provision of a hot breakfast and freshly baked goods are cited as two of the main reasons people like to stay in bed & breakfasts.

When dealing with your guests there are a number of things you can do that will help you to achieve the perception of fantastic service.

Be attentive
You need to appear interested in what your guests say. Remember the information they are giving you will help you make their stay special. You do, however, need to learn how to extricate yourself from a clinging guest without leaving them thinking you don't have time for them.

> **TIP**
> Guests want to be nurtured not smothered!

Your body language

Try to match body language in a subtle way. Face your guests directly. Don't fiddle or fidget – it gives the impression of boredom and nervousness. You want your guests to feel you are both comfortable and interested.

Maintain eye contact

The majority of people will believe you are uninterested in them if you do not have eye contact with them. They may also mistrust your sincerity.

Match your tone of voice to your meaning

You need to ensure that you sound like you mean what you say, and say what you mean. A mismatch will be evident to your listener. Try to modulate your voice and match the tone to that of your guest.

Build rapport

From the first contact with your guest, take a few minutes to build rapport. This is easy to do with people you know or like; it takes real professionalism to achieve it with people you don't know or like.

You need to learn how to do it with conscious skill. The easiest way to do this is with body language. Be subtle here, matching the angle and position of the head and torso, and only approximating the position of the arms and legs as it is these that will make your mirroring obvious if you imitate your guests too closely.

Note the language your guests use and try to use similar words, matching the tone and speed of their voice.

These may sound like very simple suggestions, but they have remarkably powerful effects.

Try them out first on people other than your guests, so that when you use these skills on your guests you can also pay attention to what they are saying until your rapport-building skills for interaction become automatic.

Dress for success

Your outward appearance is a personification of how your guests will view your establishment. If you dress well and look after yourself, your guests will believe you take the same care of your establishment. You need to ensure you are always wearing 'dressy casual' or 'smart casual'. For men, that might be a pair of slacks with a casual shirt. For women, it is something you would be comfortable going to lunch in. Your hair should be clean and well groomed.

Your nails should be clean and well trimmed. For women, make-up should be subtle. You need to ensure your breath is fresh and you have an absence of body odour.

If you are serving dinner, we would suggest a change of clothes. You want to give your guests a bit of 'theatre'.

Always be aware of your attire. Primarily, it is the male partner we are concerned with here. Don't be caught out! The suitably attired female partner in the bed & breakfast venture may need to race down to the local shop to get something, and her partner, up to his eyes in gardening, says, 'If the guests arrive while you are out I will look after them.' A nice thought, but is this casual approach going to appear professional in the eyes of a paying guest?

When cleaning, wear clothes that are easy to launder, neat and do not show the dirt. Your shoes should have rubber soles in the interest of safety. Remove any jewellery when cooking or cleaning as it may be damaged by the cleaning agents and has a tendency to promote skin irritations.

Smoking

No matter what your decision is regarding smoking, you personally should not smoke inside in front of guests. You should never smoke while working. Guests will feel offended if they see you with one hand on a vacuum cleaner while the other is holding a lit cigarette. It is all about professionalism.

Behaviour

This is where your people skills come in. If your guests look like they want to be left alone, then respect their privacy. If on the other hand your guests want to chat, then remember it's your time and subsequently you may need to determine the duration. This is a skill you will need to master.

You need to always work as quietly as possible. When guests come and stay with you, they are there to relax. They will often read, sleep in or just rest. You want to minimise any negative impact you may have on them.

When it comes to conversation, there are a few golden rules.

Never talk about religion, sex or politics until it is safely established that these topics are acceptable. Don't be baited into getting into these topics with your guests. Such discussions usually end badly.

Be friendly and nice, but don't over-host – present an aura of friendliness that doesn't tip over into familiarity. Be available to your guests for helpful advice.

After breakfast is a great time to offer some suggestions about things to see and do in your area.

Never speak to your guests about your personal problems or concerns. Your guests have sometimes come away to have a break from their problems – never burden them with yours.

> **TIP**
> Recognise your guest's need for privacy.

Staff

All the following information should be true of any staff you hire, from the casual who comes in once a fortnight to help clean to a full-time chef (if you are the proprietor of a larger establishment).

Do not rush into *hiring staff*, for in the first few years of a non-established bed & breakfast you will gain considerable cost savings if you can do much of the work yourself. It is also much easier to manage staff if you have the experience of doing their type of work.

If you decide you need to hire labour you need to consider the following:

- Work out a job description with clear duties and expectations.
- Ensure that your employees understand exactly what is expected of them and that you will be performance managing them to those criteria.
- Obtain a copy of any union agreement or award from the appropriate union body.
- Develop a win-win agreement where performance will be monitored regularly and rewarded appropriately. If you need to performance manage you will then have an appropriate forum in which to do so. The ability to retain employees will serve you in good stead for the future.
- Ask your staff to bring *feedback* to their performance appraisals – from you or your partner, from a fellow staff member and from a guest or supplier.
- Train your staff regularly on different areas of your business. Everyone should have training on customer service and occupational health and safety.
- Hold a weekly staff meeting for general news and information, and for everyone to have their say. Use this forum to update your staff on your business goals and performance. This is also a great time to recognise and reward employees who are performing well.

Entering a guest bedroom

Even though it may be a room in your house, while guests are paying for accommodation it is their room. There may be a time, however, during a guests' stay that you may need to enter their bedroom to make their beds, etc.

To avoid any possible embarrassment to either party you should follow a few simple and easy rules.

Always knock on the door and wait for an answer. If after twenty seconds there is no reply, knock again. If again there is no answer, you should call out a greeting, 'Good morning/afternoon,' and enter the room. If you are there to clean the room and your guests are still there, ask them if they wish you to come back later. Don't ever knock on a room that has a 'Do not disturb' sign displayed. It is a good idea to provide these in all rooms for your guests' use – it helps you as it is a signal as to whether they wish to be disturbed.

Some B&Bs advise their guests that the host's normal procedure is to stay out of their room unless the guest has a specific need that requires someone to go in there.

Guest behaviour

You have some liberties here if your bed & breakfast is also your home. You have the right to set some rules such as how much alcohol can be consumed, noise levels, etc. How you monitor this, and to what length you wish to go, are more difficult questions.

The main reasons you may want to comment on a guest's behaviour is if it is disturbing you or other guests, if you suspect damage to your property or if you suspect some illegal activity is occurring.

If you have to confront your guests about their behaviour you should:

- Do so in person, and in private. If the problem is occurring in the guest bedroom, approach your guest there. Don't enter the room, but conduct your conversation at the door.
- Try not to sound judgemental. Instead, gently advise your guest of the nature of the complaint and the suggested behaviour. Thank them for their time and excuse yourself.

If the guest's behaviour does not improve you need to follow up your concern with the guest. Explain to the guest that it is your policy that the comfort of all of your guests is paramount, and that one individual guest cannot disturb the peace of others. Ask for the guest to show consideration to their fellow guests.

In most cases this will be enough. However, in rare cases you may have to ask the guest to leave.

If they refuse you will need to contact the police. If you have the unhappy experience of this happening, you need to ensure that you are discreet in your handling of the affair, and keep the disturbance of any other guest to a minimum.

If, on entering a room, you find damage to your property you should make a report of it and add it to your guest's bill. If the guest has already checked out you should forward an account of the damage to the offender.

Sexual harassment

It rarely occurs in the bed & breakfast environment, but you may, at some time, be the victim of sexual harassment. Sexual harassment is an unwanted sexual advance, a request for sexual favours or any unwelcome conduct of a sexual nature. Sexual harassment is not mutual attraction between two parties. Sexual harassment is against the law.

Under the sex discrimination Acts that many countries have in place, management has a duty to prevent sexual harassment and you, the employer, may be responsible if it happens to one of your employees unless all reasonable steps have been taken to prevent it.

If you are being harassed, you need to make your objections very clear to your harasser. Make a diary note about it. If your harasser tries to make fun of you or acts unaware, repeat clearly your objection and your wish that it will cease immediately. If it continues and the harasser is in your employ, that is sufficient reason for dismissal. You must contact the police if it is a criminal offence such as rape. That said, we have not heard of one case around the world where a staff member of a bed & breakfast has been the victim of any form of assault by a guest.

Neighbours

Your neighbours' feelings about your bed & breakfast venture are going to be a key to your success. They are going to be near you every day of the year, not just during the fleeting stays of your visitors.

They are not getting any financial benefit from your venture so you need to ensure that you minimise any impact on them. There are a few things you can do to make this relationship easier:

- Make sure that your guests are aware of any rights of way and do not block your neighbours' access.
- Make sure your guests know where your property ends and your neighbours' property begins.
- Try to ensure that you follow disturbance rules regarding noise.
- Take the time to get to know your neighbours.
- Take them over one of the treats you make your guests occasionally, or have them over for coffee. Little gestures like this will pay off.

Complaints

It is human nature. Occasionally you are going to have a customer who believes your best is not good enough. You need to use these complaints to your advantage; they are valuable feedback, which will enable you to refine your product. You will find that very few people will complain, but if you investigate you may find that other guests feel the same way.

Every complaint will be different, but you need to ensure that your establishment has a procedure for dealing with complaints, which everyone understands.

A correctly handled complaint can actually increase goodwill in your business. If you don't train your employees in dealing with complaints you could in effect serve to amplify the problem to a level that could substantially damage your business.

The following are some guidelines you should consider in your handling of complaints.

Don't underestimate the power of listening

Look your guest directly in the eye, face them and listen to what they have to say. It is often a good idea to offer your guest a seat. Sit down as well; you do not want to seem intimidating.

Do not take the complaint personally

Your guest will often be upset with a situation, not with you. Speak quietly.

This works very well if your guest is raising their voice. Their volume will be unconsciously lowered to match yours.

Apologise
A statement like 'I am sorry you feel that way' does not admit fault but acknowledges your guest's feelings. Do not make excuses or trivialise the complaint. The customer only wants to know you are taking the grievance seriously. Avoid being drawn into a right and wrong argument. *Even if you win the argument, you will end up the loser if you make the guest feel trivialised.*

Deal with the complaint in a timely manner
If you need to investigate the matter further, ask your guest's permission to do so. While you are investigating, offer your guest a cup of coffee.

If the complaint is about a meal, replace it. No questions asked. Bad food will leave a bad taste in your guest's mouth in more ways than one.

Keep control of the situation
The more unreasonable and irate your guest may be, the more important it is that you stay cool, calm and collected. You need to look at the encounter as a challenge – who can be the calmest, wins. Adopt a constructive, business-like attitude. This will help move the sphere of the encounter from emotion to reason.

Never patronise or humiliate a guest
This can have disastrous results, and in the event that the mistake was yours or a member of your staff's, you will be the one who will be humiliated.

Follow up
Ensure that your guest was happy with your decision. Sometimes we believe we have settled a matter appropriately only to find out, too late, that the guest was not at all happy. You must clarify the situation for mutual satisfaction.

The next step
Fixing complaints in the short term is one thing; fixing the long-term problem is just as important. In order to analyse complaints you need to put yourself in your guest's shoes and then ask yourself the following questions.

- Is the complaint justified? Is it a disagreement with your establishment's policy or with a matter of principle?
- Is the complaint genuine? Is it the result of a unique situation, a personality clash or a genuinely difficult customer? (Trust us – they do exist.)
- Is it the first time you have heard the complaint, or is this complaint a frequent one?
- Is it a problem with a person or a system?
- Is it a trivial matter that has grown in size or intensity because of neglect?

After analysing the answers to the above, you need to set up a process to prevent it from happening again. If the complaint was about a person other than yourself, you need to address the problem immediately. Use the same principles of listening and empathy that you used with your guest. Ensure, however, your staff member understands the importance of guest happiness in your business.

The importance of feedback

As we have said before, feedback, both positive and negative, can be the most important tool in the ongoing success of your business. Most guests won't express dissatisfaction directly to you, but would be most happy to fill in a *questionnaire* (see below for an example).

You can leave the questionnaire in the bedroom, accompanied by a thank-you letter and a stamped, self-addressed envelope. Your guest is given the option of leaving the questionnaire or posting it, or sending it by email after their stay. This action will demonstrate that you are interested in their considered comments.

As an incentive for filling in the questionnaire, you could offer your guests a bonus, such as 'Stay three nights, get one free', and advise them of cooking schools, fishing weekends, gourmet dinners, family fortnights, etc. that may interest them.

TIP
You might consider a quarterly, one-page newsletter that points out forthcoming events in your area that, from knowledge gained from past guests, would be of interest.

You can also advise them of events in your local community they might be interested in and any changes you may have made to your establishment (the addition of a spa bath in one of the bedrooms, for example).

Having a professional phone manner

Make sure your phone is manned as much as possible, as most guests want to speak to the proprietor of a bed & breakfast, at some stage, before they book. How you conduct yourself during that conversation will often determine whether you clinch the booking. Don't let your personal worries intrude on your telephone manner. You must always sound as if you haven't a care in the world, and you're the warmest, most caring and hospitable person imaginable. That doesn't mean that you have to pour on the syrup with a ladle – insincerity will work against you as much as being grumpy. Just be pleasant, ready to please and – be yourself.

If you have to set the answering machine, and most of us do at some time, DO record a message that reflects your character. DON'T leave a message in a morbid tone that would be more appropriate for a funeral parlour! If you can, make it mildly humorous or something that reflects the service you offer.

If you're not confident that you can record a good message, get someone who can!

JANE'S PLACE GUEST QUESTIONNAIRE

As part of our ongoing commitment to excellence, we ask that you fill in the spaces beside the questions and leave it here, or post it back to us using the reply-paid envelope. It should be mentioned that the contents are for research purposes only and will remain confidential.

As a token of our appreciation, we will place your name in our annual lucky draw for a free two-night stay in our bed & breakfast. The results of the draw will be mailed to you at the end of this year.

Name and address:

_____

_____

Phone no:

_____

Was your stay with us up to your expectations? Y/N (circle)

Please explain why:

_____

_____

_____

Was Jane's Place easy to find? Y/N

How do you believe we could improve Jane's Place?

_____

What was the purpose of your visit in our area?

_____

Have you any plans to come our way again?

_____

Will you recommend Jane's Place to your friends? Y/N

Would you be interested in receiving Jane's Place Gazette,
our quarterly newsletter? Y/N

Thank you, and please don't forget to leave this or post it in the envelope provided
to:

PO BOX 0000,
Your Town. Post Code.

Jane Blackmore

8 Housekeeping

We've said it before and we will say it again: housekeeping is the centrepiece of a successful bed & breakfast operation. Any existing host will tell you that *if you are not fond of housekeeping, and if you are not particularly good at it, then bed & breakfast is not for you.*

Look around your house. Are you one of those people for whom everything has a place? Do you regularly clean under the beds? Do you lift all your ornaments up and individually wipe them and the surface beneath them every time you clean? Do you clean around plugholes with a toothbrush? Does your house have the look of a magazine layout?

You do and it does? Good! You are exactly the sort of person who should run a bed & breakfast. You can never be too clean when operating a B&B. Cleanliness that is good enough for friends and family may not be good enough for paying guests. The two things that will destroy your reputation as a host are bad beds, and therefore a bad night's sleep, and a 'dirty' house.

Remember that your idea of a clean house may not be the same as your guests'. Think of Felix Ungar of *The Odd Couple* – he was the neat freak. Now multiply him tenfold. That is the standard you need to reach.

Even though your guest has chosen bed & breakfast for its 'homely' atmosphere, what they actually want is the picture-book version of home. They want everything to be spotlessly clean and sparkling. They don't want to be reminded of the hundreds of guests who have stayed in the room before them. They want to feel that the room is as good as new. Immaculate cleanliness is the best way to achieve this and it will win you brownie points in the word-of-mouth stakes.

TIP
Uphold a visible standard of cleanliness!

TIP
If you don't like cleaning or ironing don't get into this business!

TIP
When cleaning watch for small details as the big things always get done.

Being prepared

When getting ready to clean, ensure that you are suitably attired. Wear flat, rubber-soled shoes and gloves. Be very careful when emptying rubbish bins, as you do not know what people can leave behind.

Having a cupboard in your laundry designated for cleaning products is a good idea. Ensure that you know what chemicals are in each product and the treatment in the event of accidental poisoning.

> **TIP**
> Cloths: use different colours for different purposes: one for the floor, one for washing up, one for wiping vegetable chopping boards, one for wiping meat chopping boards, etc.

A cleaning checklist

We would suggest that you create a checklist for cleaning each room. This will serve as a reminder that you have covered everything when setting up for your guest, and as a guide for any outside help.

Taking care of your furniture

You need to remember that your furniture has now also become the property of your guests. They, however, may not take as good care of it as you would. Thus, it becomes your responsibility to take care of it enough for all of you. The following are some hints to help you do this.

- Take care to handle your furniture carefully. Bumps and scrapes will mar wooden furniture. When you need to vacuum or mop the floors, it is better to move the furniture.
- Any spills should be wiped immediately.
- Provide plenty of coasters on coffee tables, bedside tables, lamp tables, etc., and encourage guests to use them.
- Wipe furniture daily.
- Have your couches professionally cleaned regularly.
- A good cleaning fluid does wonders on most surfaces, including granite.
- Put adhesive felt on the bottom of ornaments to protect the surface of your furniture.

> **TIP**
> Sticky marks on furniture can be removed by one tablespoon of vinegar to one litre of water.

Outside

Keep paths free from weeds and overgrown plants, and remove and replace plants as need dictates. Gardens need to be tended and your guests will appreciate the care you take of their sanctuary (and yours)!

Check outdoor lighting nightly to ensure the bulbs are functioning.

TIP

Check around the house for cobwebs each day and remove them straight away.

9 Occupational Health and Safety

It is your duty to yourself, your family, your employees and your guests to provide a safe place in which to live, work and stay. To help facilitate this we suggest you set down a few guidelines that will cover fire safety, work practices and general instructions for guests.

Fire safety

The first step is to contact your local fire authority and ask them to come out and do a fire-risk assessment.

There are different fire stipulations in different countries. For example, in some countries, B&Bs do not come under any fire precaution rules. Other countries require properties that accommodate more than six people (guests *or* staff), or if they have any sleeping accommodation above the first floor or below ground-floor level, to have a fire certificate. In some jurisdictions, fire-rating compliance is required for any number of rooms.

Follow your local fire-authority instructions to the letter and have them train you, your family and your staff on the use of your smother blanket and fire extinguisher, which you are required to provide in the kitchen and common areas. Recommendations will involve such procedures as smoke alarms in every guest bedroom, in your own bedrooms, outside your kitchen and in hallways. Having a heritage-listed home may give you a bit of leeway in the placement of alarms. You cannot legally, or morally for that matter, operate a bed & breakfast without smoke alarms.

> **TIP**
> Don't forget a fire extinguisher and a fire blanket in the kitchen.

Go around your house and replace any double adaptors with power boards. Double adaptors can be a main cause of domestic fires. Your insurance agent may also have certain requirements as part of your policy. Ensure that you adhere to any requirements.

As guests check in, draw their attention to your exits, the storage places for your smother blankets and your fire extinguishers. Advise your guests of a common meeting place outside the property in the event of a fire.

Leave your reservation diary near the door at night so you can easily check everyone off and ensure all are safe.

Never deadlock your door while you or guests are inside. In the case of a fire, you or your guests may not be able to escape.

A safe place to stay

Room by room, you need to establish that your house is as safe as it can possibly be.

In the *bathrooms*, you need to ensure bathmats have non-stick backing, that the room is thoroughly disinfected after each guest's stay, that guests do not share bar soap and that no medication is kept in the bathroom. You might want to consider handrails near the bath and the shower.

The *kitchen* can be a hotbed for germs. You need to keep pets out of the kitchen and any dining areas. Any detergents and cleaning agents should be kept in a cupboard separate from food. Ensure you know how to treat poisoning or burns that can occur from oral or eye contact with any of these agents.

You should neither smoke nor eat when preparing food. Use separate cutting boards for meat and vegetables – label them accordingly. Keep fridge temperatures at 5 °C (41 °F). Cover any wounds with plasters and gloves. Ensure you reheat foods thoroughly.

Cover food prior to serving. Wear gloves when preparing food as much as practicable. These aspects will be covered in your certificate of compliance.

In *common areas*, you should ensure lighting is adequate. Ensure that all stairs have handrails. Electrical wiring should be inspected regularly. Think about installing safety switches to protect you from power surges. Ensure rugs are taped down or have a non-slip backing. If you are planning on accommodating families, particularly toddlers, you might want to consider safety plugs for power points, safety latches on low cabinets and gates for stairs. Leave emergency numbers by the phone.

Outside you should ensure your property is well lit, that paving is in good repair and that any steps are not slippery.

A safe place to work

Not only should your bed & breakfast be a safe place to stay, you need to ensure it is a safe place to work.

🏠🏠 Train your staff and your family on fire procedures and how to use extinguishers and smother blankets. Have quarterly fire drills to ensure everyone knows where the outside meeting point is.

Another safety precaution would be hepatitis B vaccinations. Hepatitis is a rapidly spreading disease in all its permutations. As you are handling both food and cleaning, it might be a good investment to have the vaccination. See your local doctor.

Wear clean clothes and rubber-soled shoes when cleaning, as you don't want to spread germs. The most important thing you can wear when you clean, however, is a pair of gloves. It will protect you from all of the bacteria that you will encounter. Use different gloves for cleaning bathrooms than you would for cleaning any other room in the house. Do not touch your face with these gloves, ever.

Safety in the kitchen

Safety in the kitchen is twofold. It is about protecting you from accidents, in the most accident-prone place in your house, and protecting you and your guests from illness, the obvious one being food poisoning.

In certain areas, you must undertake *food-handling courses* at your nearest accredited learning facility. If it is not compulsory in your area, we would still recommend you consider one of the recognised courses. They are normally only one or two days and can save you and your business a lot of anguish in the long run. They will teach you about effective hygiene practices, food storage, cleaning and sanitising, avoiding food contamination, food legislation and legal obligations.

In most countries, food safety laws and standards apply to all businesses serving food on any occasion. Guidelines normally set minimum hygiene standards with particular reference to washing facilities, utensils, storage times, temperatures and general cleaning. In some countries you must inform your local authority environmental health officer twenty-eight days before opening for business.

There are a number of things you can do that will minimise accidents in your kitchen.

- Don't rush around the kitchen. Working methodically is more productive in the long run and minimises any chance of slipping.
- Keep knives sharp and clean. Never wash them in soapy water with other items – someone is likely to cut him or herself. When sharpening knives, do it away from your body. When wiping them do so with the sharp end pointing away from you. Always use the correct knife for the job.
- Your clothing should offer protection. Long sleeves will protect your arms from steam, and aprons will protect your body and clothes from the stove and spills.
- Use a dry cloth or oven mitt when handling hot dinner plates and saucepans. A damp cloth will heat up, create steam and ultimately result in a burn. Saucepan handles should not protrude over the edge of the stove as that can create accidents. Use two hands, protected with mitts, to carry saucepans. Arrange your oven shelves before you turn the oven on. This will help stop burns.
- Mop any spills immediately to prevent slipping.

The future

Many authorities are drafting regulations, if they haven't already put them in place, for the safe provision of food as it applies to small accommodation providers. In some areas of Australia, a food register must be signed and a food diary kept if food is to be prepared in your kitchen. If you provide evening meals and want to serve alcoholic drinks, you may need a licence. One way to find out is to contact the liquor licensing authority for more information.

While absolute food safety cannot be guaranteed by regulations, it is possible to minimise the risk to public health by ensuring that the production and handling of food is more hygienic, in direct response to the proposed hazard posed. Contact your local health authority for requirements.

It is important to appreciate the significant costs attributable to food-borne disease (entire loss of business) and the savings that could be achieved as a result of the reform of food hygiene regulations. By reducing the incidence of food-borne illness, any proposed, risk-based, preventative food hygiene standards will have specific benefits for many sectors of the community.

- By using common sense and adhering to regulations, you will have fewer incidences of food-borne illness and lower associated medical costs. As a result, there will be increased consumer confidence.
- Employers will find, both in the private and public sectors, there will be less sick leave taken due to the reduced influence of food-borne illness.
- Other industry sectors, such as tourism and local businesses, will benefit through increased customer confidence.

Identify the hazards: Some hazards can be controlled, while others may be beyond our control. For example, the quality of raw materials you receive is the responsibility of your suppliers.

Identify the critical control points: These are the points at which important processes can go wrong.

The difference between a critical control point (CCP) and a hazard is that a CCP can be controlled and monitored. Temperature control in chillers and cold-rooms is a good example of a CCP.

> **TIP**
> Wash all fruit and vegetables to remove soil, bacteria, insects and chemicals.

Set the critical limits for each CCP

If you exceed these limits you could face a major problem. For example, if your cold-room were running at a temperature of 10 °C (50 °F), this would be a problem.

Monitor the CCPs: Every CCP will require monitoring to make sure you do not exceed the critical limit. With the cold-room you would need to monitor the temperature using a hand-held thermometer.

Establish corrective action: Decide what action is to be taken if the critical limits are exceeded. If your cold-room is too warm, you should adjust the temperature or call the technician.

Set up records

This is one of the most important steps because records can prove your compliance. Records are also useful in training your staff and tracking results, for example, through regularly recording the cold-room temperature on a chart.

Will my business have to comply?

Businesses that provide, produce or package food for consumption by the general public are required to comply with all existing legislation.

First aid

We believe you have a moral, if not legal, obligation to be able to provide first aid to your staff and guests. One member of your staff or family being certified is probably enough, but it should be the person who is primarily running the establishment. Everyone in the household should know and understand your establishment's procedures for handling an emergency.

One thing you must do is purchase a comprehensive first-aid kit. You need to maintain this kit and log any incidents that occur. You can purchase this on the web through St John's Ambulance.

10 Food and the B&B

In many countries, all bed & breakfasts and guesthouses are requested to register with their environmental health department, which is often attached to the local authority. This can be a requirement as set down by your local food standards agency, which in many places has only recently been established.

In essence, the main requirement is for you to keep food-handling premises clean and that all food operations are carried out in a hygienic way.

We now reach the breakfast part of the bed & breakfast. Your house is ready, your marketing and business plans are in place, and your guests are on their way. What are you going to do about breakfast?

The cooked breakfast

This is your opportunity to shine. By now your guests should have had a glimmer of your cooking with afternoon tea on the day of their arrival. However, breakfast is the meal your guests have been waiting for. Most guests will be looking forward to the traditional fry-up; that is, the famous cooked breakfast that is still so popular with many people on holiday.

Start with the basics: a few cereals, fresh fruit juice, fruit compote or fruit, freshly baked bread, conserves, speciality teas and brewed coffee. Muffins and croissants are a nice extra.

Your guests may not want all of the above, but this should be on offer. What most will want is a hot meal and something different from what they would prepare at home. Our suggestion is that you offer a few different options for the guest to choose from.

The trick here is to be imaginative. Look in the hundreds of wonderful cookbooks that are released each year and experiment with them. Don't, however, experiment with your guests. If you want to try something new, try it on your friends and family first.

There are great recipes that have a twist on the traditional. For example, eggs Benedict served on muffins with smoked salmon, French toast mixed with cinnamon sugar and orange juice, savoury pancakes and crêpes, and a fruit platter. You can run the gamut from the traditional to the experimental, but you should have fun with it.

You don't need to offer a huge variety every day. What is better is to have one or two special dishes available every day and to rotate them, so that guests who are staying more than one night have some variety. Having staples such as bacon, eggs, mushrooms and tomatoes in your cupboard will serve you well for those guests who prefer the more traditional fare.

As for quantity, you don't want to scrimp. Most guests won't be greedy, but they will want a hearty breakfast. The one disadvantage of having breakfast in your type of accommodation is that some guests will feel they should be able to eat as much as possible. You will need to factor this into your room rate/tariff.

Presentation is almost as important as the food itself. When serving your breakfast, you need to look at the aesthetic appearance of the food through the eyes of a paying guest. Take into account colour, texture and smell. The appreciation of food is through all five senses so you should ensure you consider all of them when serving your meal.

The continental breakfast

The continental breakfast traditionally consists of a croissant or Danish pastry with coffee or tea and, if you are lucky, a glass of juice. Some bed & breakfasts who offer a continental breakfast are actually providing fruit, toast, tea and coffee. We do not believe either of these options is good enough if you want to gain recognition as a superior bed & breakfast. Most guests use the occasion of staying in a bed & breakfast as an opportunity to experience a cooked breakfast – if they wanted tea and toast, they would have stayed at home.

However, the option of a simple breakfast with toast or a continental breakfast could be offered for those who desire a lighter meal.

The breakfast basket

The provision of a breakfast basket is popular with those guests who want to be out-and-about early; for example, walkers and cyclists. It can contain fresh juice, fresh fruit compotes with yoghurt, freshly baked bread with jams and conserves, butter, a thermos of tea or coffee and, often, freshly baked goods such as Danish pastries and muffins, along with the appropriate eating and drinking utensils. If there are cooking facilities, you can also supply bacon, eggs or freshly made speciality sausages.

Presentation is very important here. You won't have the opportunity to impress with your cooking, although the freshly baked goods will help, so you need to focus on how you are going to present your breakfast. Make your basket look like a gift to the guest. Linen serviettes, rolled in a decorative napkin ring, will add a special touch. Have a look in some cookbooks for ideas.

> **TIP**
> Make your breakfasts exciting. If guests stay for more than one night vary the menu so they have a selling point for you when talking to others.

Lunch

This is really up to you, and very few guests will expect it. If you do offer it, do so at an extra cost. Remember that preparing lunch for your guests will really break into your day. The amount you charge will never make up for the time you will have to spend preparing it.

A *picnic basket*, provided at an extra cost, is a popular option for the guests. This, as with the breakfast basket, is particularly popular in places where people are likely to explore the natural wonders in the surrounding area. Preparation time is much the same as for an in-house lunch, but there is little cleaning up afterwards.

Morning and afternoon tea

As we have mentioned before, it is a great idea to welcome your travel-weary guests with morning or afternoon tea. The traditional version of this is tea or coffee with home-baked goodies, such as scones or pancakes. Some B&Bs are experimenting here as well. They are welcoming their guests with cheese, dips and antipasto. The only drawback with this is it doesn't fill your house with the same aroma as freshly baked biscuits.

This is a great opportunity to catch up with your guests, find out their plans and give them some advice on your locality. You can use the opportunity to set down any house rules you might have and acquaint them with your fire escapes, etc.

If you have a large establishment you could provide a high tea, with dainty sandwiches and cakes, scones, a selection of wonderful teas and coffees, and even the occasional string quartet. In this way you could add some theatre to your establishment and earn some extra money, making it an open house.

Dinner

Some bed & breakfasts and guesthouses do a *weekend gourmet package*, which includes an evening meal for one or more nights. This is particularly useful if you don't have a variety of restaurants in your locality that you can happily recommend. Again, experiment with some of the wonderful cookbooks on the market and try to use as much local produce as possible. Any cookbook by local writers and cooks is a great place to start.

If your guest asks to stay in for dinner without much warning you need to do two things. Charge them, and let them know that they can only have what you happen to keep in stock, or they can have what you and your family are eating. The cost charged should reflect the meal you are serving.

If you are going to cook dinner, be sure you purchase fresh meat from a quality butcher, fresh vegetables and fruit from a quality grocer and seafood from a specialist. Don't purchase these items from a supermarket, as the quality is not consistent. You want to be remembered as the host that provided a quality meal.

Eating with guests

This is really up to you and your guests, but we don't suggest you do this. Breakfast is quite a difficult meal to serve and eat at the same time. You will also find your guests sleep in, while you will need to eat early to give you strength for the day ahead.

We have found that many guests are not very comfortable sharing breakfast tables with each other, tending to be a bit monosyllabic and uncommunicative. Of all international guests, Australians tend to be a bit shy at breakfast so let them have this meal to themselves. You might find it better to ensure you have a few separate tables where couples can have breakfast alone. Ask them for their seating preference the evening before.

If you are serving dinner there is no reason why you should not eat with your guests. It is quite likely that if your guests have chosen to eat at home, they would like some company. Don't overpower the conversation, but feel free to let your natural personality shine.

Knowing the restaurants in your area

You need to become an expert on the cafés, restaurants, pubs and bars in your area.

Restaurants are one of the most important recommendations you will be asked to give. You need to have tried the restaurants you recommend as, like it or not, you will be judged on the quality of your recommendation.

By being part of your local tourism body you will meet many of the restaurateurs in your area. You may be able to arrange a 10 per cent discount for your guests, or a free cup of coffee or even a free meal for you and your partner for every ten recommendations you send their way. Never enter into an arrangement such as this, however, unless you really believe the restaurant is up to scratch. A 'free' dinner for you is no reason to destroy your credibility. Your reputation is worth much more than that.

Presentation

It is very important that you present your food to the best of your ability. While we are passionate about increasing the professionalism of the industry, we are equally passionate about bed & breakfasts retaining their individuality, or what makes them unique. If it is your style to provide sugar in a sugar bowl, then, as long as you provide a sugar spoon, feel free to do so in your B&B. The same applies to jams and conserves. This is your home and it is these small touches that your guests will be looking forward to during their stay.

Liquor licences

In most countries, you can obtain a liquor licence to suit your needs, i.e. you may need both a premises licence and at least one member of staff to hold a personal licence in order to sell alcohol to guests.

In some countries, including the UK, local councils are responsible for licensing matters but, overall, we suggest that you contact your national/state liquor licensing authority for advice and a copy of the applicable licensing policy and the necessary application forms.

In many jurisdictions, it's important to remember that you are not entitled to sell beer unless you have a certified restaurant. Under no circumstances may spirits be sold on the premises unless the B&B or guesthouse has been granted a special restaurant licence or a full publican's licence. You may also need to complete a responsible service of alcohol course.

While it may be the practice that a glass of wine or bottle of beer is provided as part of a meal on an informal basis in a B&B or guesthouse, this amounts to a breach of the licensing code – unless it is offered gratis.

Purchasing tips

The quality of your produce will be reflected in your meal. Your guests will expect as much *fresh produce*, preferably locally grown, as possible. One of the most important things you can do before even thinking of serving up a meal for your guests is to find suppliers for all of your food needs. Good suppliers for meat, fruit and vegetables, seafood and poultry are very important – as we said before, you will rarely find the quality you need at a supermarket.

A good baker is handy, but with the proliferation of bread makers on the market there is no reason why you can't bake your own. Be aware when purchasing a bread maker that many suppress the aroma – you want the smell of freshly baked bread wafting through the house. Your guests will love it.

A delicatessen is another worthwhile find. You will be able to purchase some fantastic cheeses here, and many other great treats.

Recipe ideas
Note: A cup is 250 ml.

Nectarines in Passionfruit Syrup

SERVES 4

⅓ cup sugar
½ cup passionfruit pulp (fresh or tinned)
2½ cups water
8 white nectarines, halved and stones removed

Place the sugar, passionfruit and water into a deep, heavy-base saucepan over a medium heat and simmer for 5 minutes until slightly syrupy. Add more sugar, if necessary. Add the nectarines and simmer for 1 minute on both sides or until just soft. Place the nectarines in serving bowls, strain pips from the passionfruit syrup, pour over the nectarines. Serve warm or chilled.

Baked Peach Brioche

MAKES 8 SLICES

8 small slices of brioche or fruit bread
100 g cream cheese
3 tbsp caster sugar
1 tsp vanilla extract
4 peaches, sliced
⅓ cup of icing sugar

Place the brioche slices in a baking dish lined with baking paper or foil. Combine the cream cheese, sugar and vanilla in a bowl and spread on the brioche. Top with peach slices and sprinkle heavily with icing sugar. Bake in a preheated oven at 200 °C (390 °F) for 20 minutes or until the peaches are golden. Serve warm or cold.

Raspberry Puffs

SERVES 4

1 cup self-raising flour
½ cup icing sugar
1 tsp baking power
2 eggs
60 g butter, melted
½ cup milk
300 g raspberries
Icing sugar and lemon wedges to serve

Place the flour, icing sugar and baking powder in a bowl. Add the eggs, butter and milk and mix until smooth. Mix in the raspberries. Drop spoonfuls of the mixture into a non-stick frying pan over a medium heat and cook until the puffs are golden and puffed. To serve, sprinkle with icing sugar and a slice of lemon.

Salmon Puffs

SERVES 6

Smoked salmon
2 leeks, cleaned and cut into rings, white part only
Filo pastry, 8 sheets
Butter
Poppy seeds

Filling:
300 g ricotta
300 g Gruyère, grated
2 tbsp dill, chopped
2 tbsp capers, chopped

Mix the ingredients for the filling. Brush every second sheet of filo pastry with soft butter. Layer in an ovenproof dish or in individual muffin tins: 2 sheets of buttered pastry, filling, leeks and salmon. Top with 2 layers of pastry, brush with butter and sprinkle with poppy seeds. Bake 200 °C, 40 minutes for the large pie, 20 minutes for the individual pies.

Omelette

SERVES 4–6

1 red (bell) pepper
6 slices prosciutto, roughly chopped
3 spring onions (scallions), thinly sliced
40 g feta, crumbled
40 g Parmesan, grated
4 free-range eggs
150 ml milk
1 tsp olive oil

Cut the pepper into small flat pieces and place under a hot grill until the skin blackens and blisters. Place in a bowl. Cover tightly with cling film (plastic wrap), leave for 10 minutes then rub off the skin and discard. Cut the pepper into thin strips. Heat the olive oil in a frying pan and sauté the prosciutto until crisp. Whisk the eggs and milk together, and pour into an oiled, ovenproof pan. Scatter the pepper, prosciutto and onions over the egg mixture and sprinkle Parmesan on top. Bake at 180 °C (350 °F) for 30 minutes or until the omelette is just set.

Easy Breakfast Puff Pie

SERVES 4

½ cup chopped onion
½ cup chopped courgette (zucchini)
2 oz cooked ham steak, cubed
1¼ oz grated cheddar cheese
2 tbsp sour cream
2 eggs (or 3 egg whites), beaten
Pinch pepper

Preheat the oven to 180 °C (350 °F). Spray a 9-inch pie plate with non-stick spray. Spray a frying pan with non-stick spray; add onion, courgette and ham. Cook for about 2 minutes until the onion is translucent. Beat the egg and the sour cream together, add to the other ingredients and spread on the bottom of the pie plate. Sprinkle the cheese on top. Bake until golden brown and puffy (35 to 45 minutes).

Be as flexible as possible when it comes to *breakfast serving times*. Some guests like to take the opportunity to get up early, while others like to sleep in. There is no harm, however, in asking your guests for an approximate time on the evening before so you can plan your day, or in letting your guest know when you plan to finish serving breakfast.

Like everything you do in this most competitive of businesses, your breakfasts must be first class. If you serve ordinary white bread and jams in sachets, long-life milk and a variety of cereals in little cardboard packets, you can be sure that if your guests do come back it won't be for the breakfasts!

Even if you consider yourself the world's worst cook, with a little help and imagination you can still come up with a great breakfast. You may have access to a really good bakery. If you do not, have a go at baking yourself. With bread machines and good-quality flours available, there's no excuse for serving the bland, packaged breads that abound. Baking bread is not too hard and your guests will appreciate the effort. The same goes for jams and marmalades. If you don't fancy trying to make your own, there's nearly always a little old lady nearby who makes wonderful preserves. A little research and effort on your part will pay dividends.

And remember, there's nothing wrong with bacon and eggs. Even if it isn't new and trendy, it's for good reason that it's the singular most enduring breakfast dish in the world! Just make sure the eggs are good and fresh and the bacon is top quality. These days there are any number of providers who make wonderful sausages and who will ensure delivery almost anywhere.

A recent survey indicated 95 per cent of people enjoyed a cooked breakfast but 94 per cent rarely ate one. When people go on holiday, however, they like to start the day with a cooked breakfast, so be prepared to oblige.

TIP

To check if an egg is fresh, drop it gently in a glass of cold water. If it sinks it is fresh, but if it bounces up, it is not and it should not be used.

TIP

If all else fails, start baking. It fills the house with a lovely aroma.

11 Day-to-day Operations

So, your guests are here. You have your people skills off pat. You have established a business model that works for you. What you now need to do is look at the best way to run your business day to day. You need to establish systems that will allow you to enjoy your new lifestyle, and provide your guests with a fantastic holiday experience.

Bookings

We talked in an earlier chapter about the things you will need to communicate to prospective guests over the phone and the internet. What we need to now talk about are the bookings themselves, primarily how you are going to record them.

For those of you starting your own bed & breakfast, we would suggest you begin with a *diary*. Divide each day into the number of rooms you have available. As you take bookings you should record the following information in the box for the appropriate room:

- the date you took the booking;
- the arrival and departure dates of your guest;
- the guest's name, address and phone number;
- deposit information;
- any comments, such as particular dietary requirements, estimated time of arrival, etc.

We would also suggest you set up a *reservation chart* at the front of the diary, or on the wall of your office, near your phone. This will help you see at a glance if you have rooms free on a requested date.

It is a good idea to make your reservations in pencil, in case alterations are needed, in both the chart and the diary. Don't forget to block out days that you will not be taking guests. For later reference, place the reason next to these time-off days; for example, holiday, family time, repairs, maintenance, etc.

Any chance bookings, that is, guests who arrive without a reservation, should also be added to both the chart and the diary.

Note: Most of the international reservation platforms, including Airbnb, email you notice of a pending booking and allow you twenty-four hours to confirm that you accept the reservation. They also can handle deposits.

The other part of the booking is the *deposit*. We would suggest you take at least 25 per cent as a deposit. Many bed & breakfasts make these deposits non-refundable. You must specify this at the time of booking. For holidays and other busy times, we suggest you take a larger deposit. Another good idea is to have minimum stays, for example three nights, for events and long weekends. This will ensure your occupancy is high and you don't miss out on other bookings during a peak period.

> **TIP**
> Have a cancellation policy and be prompt with refunds if applicable.

Airbnb collect the payments from the guests and remit the same to you minus 3 per cent commission within twenty-four hours of the guest's arrival.

Guest registration

Guests may not have any obligation to provide you with their permanent address, but we would suggest you ask for this, not least for the database you can then create to use for marketing at a later date.

Up until a few years ago, an exercise book was sufficient for registration purposes, but every year the level of professionalism in this industry is rising and it is this professionalism your guests will remember. They don't want to necessarily check in as if they were staying in a hotel, but an old exercise book is not really good enough.

So, what are the options? There are two main forms of registration. One is the use of a *guest register* and the other is the individual *registration form* or card.

Guest register

This is a bound book, divided into columns, which your guests fill in upon arrival. Guests from overseas may need to fill out the country of residence and passport number and, in some cases, their next destination. In this situation, you will need to see your guest's passport.

In some countries, there is a legal requirement for larger establishments to keep a record of the full name and nationality of all guests over the age of sixteen. Records in this situation must be kept for a minimum of twelve months. We suggest you contact your local authority for the legal requirements in your area.

The guest register is popular because all the details are in one place and in chronological order, making it easy for referral, and it is very inexpensive as each guest only takes up one line in the register. The downsides are that it can become tatty from overuse and illegible if guests make mistakes, and it is indiscreet, as your guests can easily see the personal details of other guests.

Individual registration form or card

The individual registration form or card performs the same functions as a register. It is more expensive than a register as each guest has an individual card or form, but you can generate these forms easily from your computer. This format is discreet, as no one except you and your guest sees the form. It is neat: if a guest makes a mistake, you can provide a new one, and it can be filed easily. It also has space for both you and your guest to make comments (dietary, special requirements, etc.), which can be valuable information for later visits.

Insurance

Regardless of whether your business is in your home, on your property, around the corner, leased by you or a variation on these themes, insurance is one of the most important considerations you will have when running your bed & breakfast. It has the potential to protect your home and lifestyle in a way nothing else can – against the unexpected! After all, who can be properly prepared for the unexpected?

Insurance is a very simple concept. For an annual payment, an insurance company agrees to provide specific cover for your *building and contents and other B&B specific areas, including liability to your paying guests.* Many insurers provide the facility to spread payments by direct debit, although there is likely to be a charge for this.

Even if you believe you have adequate funds to replace or repair any loss that could occur, consideration must be given to investing in a suitable insurance policy.

In fact, in our increasingly litigious society, it would be irresponsible not to be adequately insured. Remember, as a host, you have a responsibility not only to yourself and your family, but also to your guests.

So, what constitutes adequate insurance in your specific case (one of the beauties of B&Bs is that you are all different from each other). Let us identify and evaluate the major areas of risk.

The biggest risk, in fact, may be the general public themselves.

You have people coming to your home or property you do not know and who do not know you. You cannot guess how they look after their own possessions, so how can you know how they will look after yours?

Most B&B guests are the loveliest of people and some become life-long friends. Some, however, you will never please and you will wonder why they came in the first place. Things get broken, perhaps, but no one confesses. Perhaps your lovely guest robes disappear when the guests leave. How do you handle situations like this and remain hospitable and content?

There are tricks of the trade concerning small losses and other operators will share some of these with you. Although your insurance policy should allow for claims of this nature, you may be penalised for making small claims continually. You need to realise that insurance companies are businesses as well. An insurer has the right to decline to renew a policy, or even to quote in the first instance, if they feel you are a bad risk; for example, if you make a lot of little claims on a continual basis.

Only you alone know your property intimately. Guests do not. In the dark, or in a strange place, people can get hurt.

They don't know that the stairs are a little uneven or the coffee table is close to the sofa because the room is narrow. Perhaps they slip on a rug on the polished wooden floor, or in the night run into a piece of furniture or fall down the stairs. You will need to look at your property through the eyes of a stranger and try to determine any potential risks. This is called *risk management*.

You can protect yourself against these risks by taking out appropriate insurance coverage. The word 'appropriate' is important as many B&Bs pay for insurance each year, but don't have the cover they thought they had. Even worse, some do not have cover at all.

How can this be? Well, the first and most important thing to remember is that in most cases your current householders' policy WILL NOT COVER YOU. Be aware that many insurers do not insure B&Bs at all. This is not the negative it implies. If an insurance company doesn't understand what it is insuring, it is highly unlikely it will provide you with the type of policy you will require. If in doubt, ask questions!

One of the most important conditions of any policy is the 'duty of disclosure'. For instance, your 'duty' would be to inform your current insurer once you decide to have paying guests or run a business from your home. This would also extend to long- or short-term paying students and to workers.

You have an obligation to advise your insurance company of this and of any alterations you make to your home. Advising an insurance company in writing about the change from homeowner to B&B owner is imperative. It provides your insurers with accurate information and obliges them to confirm or decline your existing policy. Doing this in writing also provides some protection.

Firstly, you have a copy with details of when and to whom it was sent; secondly, written correspondence generally provokes a written response. This helps to protect you and substantiates basic information in the event of a dispute.

When writing to insurers, be clear and specific and ask them for written confirmation for all areas of your cover, checking that all the elements of your domestic policy, if you had one, still cover your new circumstances.

You will need to advise your insurer of:

- The number of guests for which you have facilities.
- What specific changes you might make to your home; for example, renovations.
- Whether you have a restaurant; and any plans to serve morning or afternoon teas to guests or to the general public.
- Whether you will be serving or providing alcohol and any licences you may have that permit this.
- Whether you run any other business from your home or property. Many householders' policies exclude the running of any business from their home.
- Whether you employ staff, perhaps a gardener or casual cleaning person. If you are running a B&B and pay people to work for you, you are no longer a domestic situation and your domestic policy, if you have one, will not cover you.
- What sort of activities you provide for your guests. Are you on a farm and have the guests interacting with farm animals or other aspects of farm life?

Many insurers neither understand nor wish to insure B&B accommodation and will tell you that quite clearly. Some may offer separate liability policies. That may solve one aspect of your insurance needs, but what does it mean for your building and contents cover?

Perhaps they will offer to cover your home under a combined domestic and business policy. This can leave building and contents with very different, and usually less, cover than you have enjoyed under a householder's policy.

This combined type of insurance cover requires you to pick and choose each section of cover, for example, glass, fire, money and burglary, and then pay extra for basic covers that would be automatically included in a specialist B&B policy.

Buying separate liability policies is expensive and can mean you have two or three different insurance companies covering your needs. If something happens, are these providers easily able to work together or will there be problems determining who is responsible for what because of the mishmash of policies put together like a patchwork quilt? You are also likely to have an excess (deductible) under each policy – whereas only one excess is likely to apply if you have a specialist policy.

If you have a farm and already have one or other of these policies, *do not* assume it extends to your B&B as well. It probably won't, unless you have specifically arranged for it to do so.

What cover do I need to consider?

Public & Private Liability is a MUST. It refers to the general public in a business sense. It relates to injury and property damage caused by your personal negligence and/or business negligence (where you are proven to have been negligent – it also covers the cost of defending such claims). If part of your property is not well maintained and clear of debris, a guest may fall and sustain an injury.

We suggest that you have the equivalent of £/€/$10–20 million public/private liability cover.

Product Liability relates to any products you provide, but is especially relevant to the food you serve. It doesn't matter whether you bought it from the bakery or not, should a guest find something 'extra' in it, you are liable.

Employers' Liability – once you know that you are going to employ staff, be they full-time, part-time or casual cleaners, chefs or gardeners, talk with your insurance broker in detail about employers' liability insurance. This is compulsory in the UK and may be automatically covered by your home insurance.

Buildings & Contents Cover – your building and contents insurance should reflect true replacement values. If you have more than one building, it is advisable you show each building and its contents separately. Insurance is not based on a market value or saleable value. It is based on replacing or repairing. If you are unsure of the costs, it is wise to ask a builder or valuer to provide you with an estimate based on your property. Add to that a percentage or lump sum allowance for removal of debris, architect's fees and council requirements, to name a few of the additional costs. Please bear in mind the building regulations applicable to listed properties. You should pay particular attention to ensuring that you have adequate cover.

Insurers will be interested in the construction of your property. Usually, standard construction is considered to be homes built from brick, stone, slate or tile. If your property is built from other materials then please notify the insurer. You should also say if any part of it has a flat roof.

Be aware that you should discuss with your builder any requirements for covering work carried out, should you need to repair or renovate.

The best way to protect yourself in this respect is to employ a well-known builder with a good reputation. He should carry his own insurance and be happy to show evidence of this to you.

Most buildings policies will also cover the cost of alternative accommodation for the policyholder and their family while the main premises are not habitable. The level of cover does vary but this could prove to be an important aspect of cover in the event of a major loss.

When assessing your contents cover, have special regard for antiques, valuables and other high-risk portable items such as cameras, laptops and jewellery. Some insurers may ask you to improve the security of your home (for example, by fitting a safe) if these items form a high proportion of your overall cover. It is a good idea to collate a list of these and keep photographic evidence/receipts for any valued over £/€/$2000.

Alternative Accommodation and Rent – this section is likely to be a benefit of a specialist B&B policy. It will cover the additional costs you incur for alternative accommodation while your home is uninhabitable following a major loss.

Loss of Board & Lodgings – this will compensate you for loss of income for pre-booked accommodation up to a maximum amount, for example £/€/$8500.

Full Theft Cover – most standard household policies will exclude theft unless by forcible and violent entry.

Full Accidental Damage Cover – this cover means that your insurer will not be able to come back to you when you want to claim for a broken window or a cracked washbasin and say, 'Prove to us a guest did not do it!'

There are very few insurance companies who provide a B&B specific policy. Those who do, generally provide this through an insurance broker. In the main, you will find this specialised cover is available as a specific scheme managed by that broker.

Don't rely on your current insurance broker to find a specialist B&B insurance provider for you. The best place to find out about these people is through a referral from another B&B owner, your regional tourist board or from one of the B&B associations. Nowadays the internet is readily available to many B&B owners, as it is becoming an increasingly popular way to advertise their B&Bs. Try using a search engine by typing in the phrase 'bed & breakfast insurance' to locate B&B insurance providers.

These insurers will still have differences between the coverage they offer and their service and involvement in the industry, but the cover will be specific to the B&B industry. Don't be afraid to get different quotes and ask as many questions as you can. This allows you to make educated decisions and buy as directly as possible.

For more, see Ryan's Hospitality Division (www.ryans.co.uk).

Payment

There is no set way of handling this part of your interaction with your guests. Some B&Bs prefer to settle the account at the beginning of the stay, particularly if you do not have extras that the guest can choose during their stay, while others keep to the traditional way of paying at the end. It is your establishment – the way you run it is up to you.

Either way, you will need to present your guest with an *itemised account*, retaining a duplicate yourself. This could be in the form of a handwritten invoice – you can buy invoices at your local stationers – or a computer-generated account, printed with your letterhead, so you can store your record electronically.

Methods of payment

There are many different options for payment and you will need to decide which you will choose to accept. You might like to discuss your options and the positives and negatives of each with your financial advisor, accountant or bank consultant. It is a good idea to list your payment options on your promotional literature.

Cash

Despite the surge in online payment functionality, the acceptance of cash is still a viable option for any business because of the cleared funds aspect to cash and the immediate liquidity it provides your business on a day-to-day basis. The only negatives are that you may be charged a small deposit fee and you will need a safe to store the money until you can go to the bank.

Cheques

Many establishments choose not to accept cheques, but some of your guests may expect this facility. Some guests may wish to pay by personal cheque either in local currency or in foreign currency.

This method of payment is high-risk and fraud can easily occur; it is also not recommended because personal cheques can be 'stopped' or 'returned' for varying reasons and at a later date. Cheques are now very easily falsified. If a personal cheque is returned it will mean that you, the B&B owner, would be out of pocket for the duration of the stay that the payment originally covered. If you do accept cheques, then be sure to view the guest's cheque guarantee card, credit or debit card, or driver's licence, and record the guest's details on the reverse side of the cheque. If your guest is from another country, record their passport number and details as well. Ensure any alterations are initialled, and the cheque is not post-dated, and also ensure the payer name on the cheque is that of your guest, and the payee name is the same as the account into which you will be depositing.

With the number of cash machines now available, it is reasonable to assume that cash will be the favoured method of payment. However, international guests are more than likely to use their credit card or may have already paid in advance using an online payment method.

Credit and debit cards

Many of your guests will want to settle their account by this method. The financial size of your establishment will probably make the difference as to whether you choose to accept credit or debit cards. If you choose to go down this route there are a few things you will need to do.

Firstly, you need to apply for merchant card status from your bank. For the privilege of using their service, you will pay a commission of around 2–5 per cent of the face value of the payment. You will be given a limit, which covers the payment for the duration of the guest's stay. Any charge after that will require an authorisation number. When applying for merchant card status be sure to have a telephone facility. This will allow you to take a non-refundable deposit. The hardware required is multi-functional in that it accepts both credit- and debit-card transactions.

It operates off either modem-based technology through a phone line or wi-fi. The set-up costs, excluding the multi-functional hardware, could be quite expensive, but it is worthwhile if your property is a large guesthouse. Talk to your bank representative to ascertain all of the costs.

Traveller's cheques

Some overseas guests still use this form of payment instead of credit or debit cards.

Traveller's cheques in foreign currency will require you to convert them in your country's currency, e.g. sterling. The exchange rate the bank will use to convert these instruments may have an 8–12 per cent margin loading; therefore, ensure that you have factored this into your pricing. End-cashing traveller's cheques can be quite problematic because your bank must be comfortable accepting and negotiating third-party cheques irrespective of the brand of traveller's cheque. And be aware of hidden bank charges, which may indeed be debited from your bank account long after your guest leaves your premises.

Again, discuss this type of payment with your bank representative first. You will need to ensure that your guest produces suitable identification, e.g. a passport, and signs the cheque in front of you. Be sure to record the passport number and details on the reverse side of each traveller's cheque and be aware of any fraudulent activity. If the cheque looks fake, DO NOT accept it.

Foreign currency cash

If you choose to accept foreign currency cash, you will need to convert it into your country's currency and add the service fee the bank will charge you. Be aware that banks and brokers will factor in a 10–15 per cent margin loading, plus a fee for accepting and converting foreign currency. Ensure that you have factored this into your pricing. You must ensure you get the exchange rate from your bank. Get the money to the bank that day, otherwise you may lose money on the transaction if the exchange rate changes. Try to encourage your guests to change the money themselves as this will negate the additional expense at your bank.

Online payment solutions

Of the now many payment gateways available to you via online capabilities worldwide, PayPal has a web-based program that enables anyone with an email address to easily send and receive secure payments online. PayPal is an eBay company specialising in online payment solutions with more than eighty-six million account members worldwide. It operates in fifty-six countries and supports six currencies – pounds sterling, euros, Australian dollars, US dollars, Canadian dollars and Japanese yen.

Payments from bookings via the international reservation platforms are paid into your bank account minus their commission.

Discuss with your bank the feasibility of online banking and online payment gateways.

Pre-paid vouchers

Another form of payment that you may have to think about is the pre-paid voucher. Many tour operators and other agencies issue these to their clients who then hand them to their B&B host in exchange for a night's stay. The accommodation may be pre-booked for an additional fee or on a use-as-you-go basis.

This arrangement has to be formally agreed months in advance. The B&B host normally posts the used voucher to the issuing agency for payment.

Systems can vary from company to company and there are usually additional agreements about supplements for extras of one kind or another, such as children sharing superior accommodation, which must be paid directly to the host by the guest on the spot.

You may be approached individually about this type of business or it could be one of the many options open to you as a member of a consortium or B&B association. Either way, you should discuss it fully with others already in the system before committing yourself. There is normally no cost involved for those agreeing to participate in voucher transactions. However, there may be a commission payable at some stage in the process. Check your voucher issuer for their procedure.

Travel agents are encouraging clients to purchase pre-paid accommodation vouchers before they leave home. This has resulted in an increase in the use of vouchers. The B&B voucher business is big and growing, especially among bed & breakfast hosts who are well organised and belong to their own associations. This is particularly the case throughout Ireland where a truly vast B&B voucher business has been painstakingly built up and finely tuned over the past thirty years or so.

The flexibility of B&B voucher programmes is very appealing to international visitors travelling around the UK and Ireland. Discover Travel & Tours is very well known within the international travel trade and is always looking for quality B&Bs, inns and guesthouses to join their programme.

Financial records

You need to keep records of your bed & breakfast's financial performance primarily for taxation purposes, but also to help monitor your business's growth. *Value Added Tax/Goods and Services Tax records*, or similar depending on the country, are required to be kept by all registered business operators. As we have said many times in this publication, it would be wise to contact a financial advisor prior to deciding anything to do with your bed & breakfast. The Inland Revenue or its equivalent, in particular, is a fount of information. You are legally required to keep your records for taxation purposes and the tax office may be able to provide you with a CD-ROM designed for this purpose.

Sage, or a similar computer program, is a worthwhile investment for record-keeping and for tracking your business activities. Due to the complexities of tax systems, we will not be going into great depth on the records the government requires you to keep. Other than recommending that you contact the Inland Revenue, we would suggest you apply to your closest VAT/GST office for registration if required. Customs and Excise or, in the UK, Her Majesty's Revenue and Customs (HMRC) administer this office. A VAT/GST-registered business must show its number on all literature and documentation pertaining to the business.

As for the figures, you need to assess your financial progress. We would suggest that every month you reconcile and look at the following:

Accommodation cash flow

This is the permanent record of your occupancy and income. With this information, you can compare month-to-month, year-to-year trading, highlighting regular seasonal highs and lows and allowing you to forecast accurately. You can then turn this information into graphs, perhaps even comparing weekend and weekday trade, to plan for the coming year or season. As the months go by, you will be able to make decisions on when your busiest periods are, enabling you to market to fill in the gaps or pinpoint the best time for you to take a well-earned break.

Operating expenses

These are the fixed costs each month, such as leases, rent, rates, insurance, loans, memberships, etc; plus your variable costs, such as telephone, electricity, gas, water, labour (including your own), food, decoration, etc. Again, graphs are a great tool for comparison and can help determine whether further investigation is needed. For example, one month you may have spent £/€/$300 on food, while the next you only spent £/€/$210, but your accommodation receipts were similar. Ask yourself what changed.

Break-even analysis

The combination of your operating expenses and your accommodation cash flow provides you with the material to prepare a break-even analysis. When your costs are higher than your income, you are running at a loss. Break-even is the point when the two meet, and all income above that is profit.

Bank balance

Another long-term indicator is the comparison between your opening and closing bank balance each month. It helps track your expenditure and is also good to convert to graph form.

Debtors and creditors

Monthly reconciliation of the money owed to you by debtors, and by you to creditors, is imperative when running a successful business. Ensure that you pay by your due date, as you want to maintain a good credit rating, particularly if you are part of a small community. You should ensure you put in place a process to follow up debtors. While they are not paying you, you are losing valuable interest.

Profit and loss statement

This is the conclusion of all of the above. Subtracting your costs from actual sales revenue from accommodation receipts will give you a gross profit estimate for the month. Then subtract all other costs including a pro rata amount for variable expenditure. This will give you a net profit figure.

The net profit is the bottom-line figure from which you can draw cash, pay off capital or retain cash in the business for future growth. It is also the figure you can match against the value of your business assets to see the return on your investments.

With all these figures at your fingertips you can build an accurate picture of the financial position of your business. Recording these figures each month gives you the ability to keep your business finely tuned. You will be able to see trends in profits, costs and sales. It will also help you to see any potential problems if one or more of these indicators begin to go off track.

A business will eventually fail if it is not profitable. It may also fail even if it is profitable on paper, but when cash flow is not monitored to ensure that debts are paid when due or you take too much cash out of the business.

General ledger

A general ledger is a day-by-day record of your daily incomings and outgoings. In any business, including B&Bs, you need to ensure a general ledger is established and maintained in order to monitor debits and credits against each salient item. An accountant or financial advisor is the best person to assist you in setting up your books, in particular your general ledger. Again, a suitable commercial computer program can help you here.

Banking

It is imperative, for both security and financial reasons, that you put your payments into the bank as quickly as possible.

If you are unable to get to your bank every day, and have the potential to carry large sums of money on your premises, you must inform your insurance company. We would also suggest the installation of a small safe.

A meeting with your bank manager would be a good idea when starting up your business. Your bank should be able to advise you of the best accounts to run your business and will provide you with the necessary documentation that will need to accompany any transaction.

To make your time at the bank more efficient:

- always sort coins and notes into denominations and place like coins in the bags provided by the bank;
- list your cheques on the deposit slip; and
- pay your foreign currency to the bank using a separate slip.

Don't forget that for credit-card transactions there is nothing to bank as the payments are electronic. Debit-card transactions go straight into your account.

If you are unable to get to the bank during trading hours, find out if the bank has a *night-safe facility*. The bank will be able to issue you with a commercial wallet in which to put your money. The bank will also give you a key or a code that will unlock the night safe.

If your guest booking is via Airbnb, then payment for the total amount minus their 3 per cent commission is deposited into your account twenty-four hours after the guests have departed.

TIP
Make sure your customer is satisfied even if you can't personally help them. For example, if you have no available accommodation on the given night, refer them to someone who can help them.

12 The Hospitality Industry and You

The important thing to remember as you start this journey is that you are not alone. You are part of a larger entity called the hospitality industry. Much of your success will be down to your ability to work cooperatively with others in the industry both here and overseas.

The structure of tourism authorities

All countries have national and regional tourism boards that, in essence, take responsibility for the developing strategies that ensure their share of tourist revenue.

In many countries those registered with their local tourist association may well find they get a lot of their bookings from this source, either by direct bookings through the association or through a listing in their official publication.

For the reasons mentioned above, we urge everyone in the bed & breakfast industry to join their respective tourism organisation, board or association (in some places, some form of membership is compulsory). This will help you to identify why tourists visit your area, to network with other B&B operators, to access local information that helps you make better target-market decisions, and to keep you up to date with tourism development. Be proactive not reactive.

We advise you to search online the names of the various tourist structures in your country along with their contact addresses. You can also find out the membership entry levels in order to gain other valuable industry contacts.

Local tourist organisations

If you have not yet got the picture that you need to be actively involved in the tourism community, we have failed. Your local tourism authority is probably the most important organisation you can join. It will provide you with vital information about your market, but most importantly it will give you vital contacts. Local tourism operators thrive off interaction with each other. It really is a case of: you scratch my back and I'll scratch yours.

Bed & breakfast associations

B&B associations are set up as advisory organisations on their members' behalf and subsequently cover current trends, regulations (be they health and safety or local government) and insurance, to name just a few areas, that impact on the B&B accommodation industry. To that end, we recommend you join your state/national B&B or farmstay association, which can be found by searching on the internet.

Reservation platforms

There are several international reservation platforms, such as Airbnb, Stayz, Windu, TripAdvisor, Booking.com and Onefinestay, that encourage you to list your property on their websites. These services are popular with consumers; the shared economy (i.e. peer-to-peer online transactions) is changing the way in which people book their accommodation and the way in which accommodation houses, and in particular B&Bs, receive bookings.

Most international reservation platforms that list B&B properties inform the owners that they should adhere to local government regulations. Property owners place themselves at risk if anything goes wrong, such as personal accidents, while hosting guests and if they have inadequate public liability cover and no or limited fire-safety precautions.

Destination marketing

Destination marketing plays an integral part in the marketing of tourism products. Whether the product is an attraction, an activity, scenery or a bed & breakfast, they all, collectively, form the essence of the destination. The more popular the destination, the better are the chances for individual tourism operators to promote and sell their products to potential customers in a cost-effective way.

Destination marketing, promoting the unique brand of a destination, is one of the tasks with which local or regional tourism organisations are charged. They prepare the base from which individual operators can undertake their own marketing and promotion at a reduced cost.

Locations such as Lucca and Siena or Katoomba may not mean a lot to many people, nor would they necessarily associate them with any type of holiday experience. Mention the destination brand, Tuscany or the Blue Mountains, and the story is different. Many will associate that brand not only with a very specific holiday expectation, but they can also place it geographically.

In other words, if the destination is known in the marketplace or if it has brand identity, each individual business has the chance of being seen in its marketplace and to reach potential customers faster and at a lesser cost.

It should be in everyone's interest, from the smallest B&B operator to the largest attraction, to ensure that your local and regional tourism organisations receive sufficient support to undertake destination marketing, promote the region and create brand awareness. In return, individual businesses will benefit.

B&B classification

We take the view that the two-party property review programme that most international reservation platforms use is not always reliable. We have booked into many diverse listed properties in order to measure their level of hospitality along with the presentation and facilities offered to the paying guest, and have compared these to the reviews written up on the internet.

In some instances, the stay was disappointing. For example, in some properties we thought we were going to stay in four-star properties, as rated by previous guests, when in fact the accommodation provided would not have made a two-star rating under the legitimate star-rating system as put in place by the official body in the appropriate country.

We firmly believe that the two-party (review) rating idea, in which the visitor and the host rate the property and which is promoted by the international reservation platforms, is not very credible on a standalone basis. The problems are that the review guests give the property is mostly an emotional one and the same might also apply to the owner's rating of the guest. Currently there are no parameters established so that consequently there is little consistency in the rating process.

Ideally, the three-party system is used when rating the property. This is a tried and tested way for the prospective guest to know what the standard is likely to be (with no surprises). Guests should be able to provide a review, but not be expected to rate the property as a sole indicator of the facilities on offer.

Note: The three-party grading system involves the property owner, the guest and the grading inspector who uses a specially designed system to appraise each accommodation type. The two-party rating system only involves the property owner and the guest.

We advise B&B owners to be rated by your country's legitimate star-rating system, i.e. a *national accommodation classification scheme* that is supported by regional tourist bodies, and to show your star rating on the reservation platforms when listing your property.

The key requirements at rating levels are usually as follows:

One-star rating

There is a minimum entry requirement for achieving a one-star rating:

- A cooked breakfast or substantial continental one.
- Owners/staff must be available for guest arrivals and departures and also meal times, i.e. breakfast.
- Once registered, guests must have free access to your property at all times unless you have made other entry arrangements with your guests.
- All serviced areas and facilities must be kept clean and maintained (minimum quality requirement), and the delivery of services should be maintained.
- A dining room or similar eating area must be available unless meals are served in the bedrooms.
- You must meet all current statutory obligations and provide public liability cover.

Two-star rating

- Courteous service.
- Well-maintained beds.
- Breakfast prepared with a good level of care.
- For self-catering, a good standard of quality overall is required, with good use of space and a wider range of facilities/items provided.

Three-star rating and above

- Access to both sides of all beds for double occupancy.
- Bathrooms/shower cannot be shared with the owner.
- A washbasin in every guest bedroom (could be en-suite).

Four-star rating

- At least 50 per cent of guestrooms to have an en-suite or private facilities.

Five-star rating:

- All guest bedrooms to have an en-suite or private facilities.

These five levels of quality ranging from one to five stars are agreed by all assessor agencies; those wishing to obtain a higher star level will need to provide enhanced quality standards across all areas with a particular emphasis on cleanliness, breakfast, hospitality, bedrooms and bathrooms. Definitions set down by the grading authorities are:

- Bed & breakfast: Accommodation in a private house, run by the owner and no more than six paying guests.
- Guesthouse: Accommodation provided for more than six paying guests and run on a more commercial basis than a B&B. Usually more services, for example dinner provided by the owners.
- Farmstay: B&B or guesthouse accommodation provided on a working farm or smallholding.

Statutory obligations

All statutory obligations must be adhered to and include the following:

- Fire precautions
- Price display orders
- Food/safety/hygiene regulations
- Licensing laws
- Health and safety regulations

- Anti-discrimination laws
- Trade description laws
- Data protection laws
- Relevant hotel proprietors laws Acts

You will most likely be asked to show clear evidence that public/private liability cover is being maintained and that the above requirements are fulfilled.

So why should you be classified?

As more people enter this market the guest is going to become more discerning. Those properties that can advertise their rating can only benefit from it.

Tourism accreditation is a process designed to establish and continually improve industry standards for conducting tourism businesses. It aims to assist every tourism business to improve the way it operates. Given that the system is third-party-graded means that it has more credibility than the two-party schemes on offer.

As a point of interest, the Onefinestay reservation platform has representatives who personally inspect each property that wants to be listed with them. The property firstly must meet their required standard.

It is important to bear in mind that the star-rating system takes into account the nature of the property and the expectation of the guests – so a farmhouse is just as entitled to five stars as a country hotel, as long as what it offers is of the highest standard.

★	Fair and Acceptable
★★	Good
★★★	Very Good
★★★★	Excellent*
★★★★★	Exceptional, world-class*

*You will be guaranteed a wider range of facilities.

Symbols

Below is a guide to symbols used, particularly for farmstays, to indicate the features and facilities available.

Symbol	Accommodation Type
	Bed & Breakfast
	Self-catering
	Bunkhouse
	Camping
	Caravanning

Symbol	Explanation
	Children welcome (minimum age)
	Dogs by arrangement
	Accommodation for disabled/less able people – check for details
	No smoking
	Smokers welcome
	Credit cards accepted
	Businesspeople welcome
	Way-marked walks on farm
	Foreign languages spoken
	Riding on farm
	Fishing on farm
	Country house, not a working farm

A rating from one star to five stars is the best way for guests to assess the quality of stay that they are looking at. Ratings are an internationally applied yardstick and are administered in this country according to very strict guidelines.

> **TIP**
> Being graded gives you an advantage over your competitors.

13 Marketing Your B&B

This chapter assists you in designing an effective *marketing plan or concept* for your bed & breakfast. This should help you come to decisions on what style of marketing (advertising, promotions, public relations and direct mail, to name just a few) will suit both your customer and your financial situation.

Marketing concept

The factor that underpins your marketing concept is the importance of guests to your bed & breakfast. All of your activities should be aimed at satisfying your guests' needs, while obtaining a profitable, rather than maximum, occupancy.

To develop a marketing concept for your bed & breakfast you must:

- determine the needs of your guests (market research);
- develop competitive advantages (marketing strategy);
- select specific markets to serve (target marketing); and
- determine how to satisfy those needs (marketing mix).

Market research

The fundamentals of operating a successful bed & breakfast are the same as running any small business. If you do your homework first then there is less likelihood of coming unstuck.

> **TIP**
> Ongoing research is a prerequisite for ongoing viability.

The aim of market research is to find out who your guests are, what they want, and where and when they want it.

This research can also expose problems in the way in which you provide products or services, and help you find areas for expansion of current services to fill customer demand. Market research should also identify trends that can affect bookings and profit levels.

Market research should give you more information than simply who your customers are. Use this knowledge to determine matters such as your market share, the effectiveness of your advertising and promotions, and the response to any new, value-added services that you have introduced.

While larger companies hire professionals to do their research, small-business owners and managers are closer to their customers and are better able to learn much faster the likes and dislikes of their guests. They are better positioned to react quickly to any change in customer preferences.

Competition

Monitoring the competition can be a useful source of information. Their activities may provide important information about guest demands that were overlooked. They may be capturing part of the market by offering something unique or different. Likewise, bed & breakfast operators can capitalise on unique points of their product that the competition does not offer.

- What is the competition's market share?
- How much revenue do you suspect they make?
- How many bed & breakfasts are targeting the same market?
- What attracts customers to them?
- What strengths do they advertise?

Trends

- Any population shifts.
- Changes in local tourism development.
- Lifestyle changes in the nearest metro city area.
- Short-break holidays taken during the week instead of only at weekends.

Market research does not have to be sophisticated and expensive. While money can be spent in collecting research material, a lot of valuable information can be accessed by the bed & breakfast operator using the following methods:

Employees

This is one of the best sources of information about guest likes and dislikes. Usually employees work more directly with guests and hear complaints that may not make it to the owner. They are also aware of items or services that guests may request and that the bed & breakfast doesn't currently offer.

Guests
Talk to your guests to get a feel for your clientele, and ask them where improvements can be made. Collecting guest comments and suggestions is an effective form of research, as well as instilling customer confidence in your product and property.

Records and files
Looking at your business records and files can be very informative. Peruse your revenue records, complaints, receipts or any other records that can show you where your guests live or work, or how and what interests them. One bed & breakfast operator found that addresses on cash receipts allowed for the pinpointing of guests in a specific geographic area. She thought clients may like to sample the similar yet different features her area offered.

With this kind of information, one can cross-reference the guest addresses and check the effectiveness of the advertising placements. You need to take into account that this material represents the past and the information that you need to determine present and future trends may mean that some past information is too obsolete to be effective, but at least you will have a general idea of what to look for.

Marketing strategy
With the research information gathered, the next step is to develop a marketing strategy. Use this information to determine areas where the competition doesn't adequately fill consumer demand, or to find areas where a new service or different promotion would capture part of the market. A new bed & breakfast may capture a significant market share by aiming its marketing strategy towards areas not focused on by the competition.

Some examples of the various areas of emphasis include offering:

- more innovative sightseeing options;
- better value for the guests, for example an emphasis on quality;

- specialised service instead of a broad one;
- modified facilities or any improvements; and
- a flexible pricing policy.

While a new bed & breakfast can enter this business and capture a share of the market, an established one can use the same strategies to increase its market share.

Target marketing

Once your marketing strategy is developed, you need to determine the customer group for which it will be most effective. For example, a 'value for money' option may appeal to the family market while 'quality and top service' would be more attractive to couples.

Another example could be offering a gift voucher that is set at a fixed denomination i.e. £/€/$100. The person who buys this pre-paid voucher might present it to a friend or family member as a gift. This allows the holder to use the voucher as payment when checking into your bed & breakfast.

Remember that different marketing strategies may appeal to different target markets. Apply the collected data to choose the combinations that will work best.

The market is defined by different segments. Some examples of this are:

Geographic
Specialise product options to suit guests who live in certain neighbourhoods or regions, or who are from different climates.

Demographic
Direct advertising towards families, retired people or the disabled, or to the occupation or profession of potential guests.

Special interest groups
Target promotions towards the opinions or attitudes of the customers (political or religious, for example).

Product benefits

Aim marketing to emphasise the benefits of the product or service that would appeal to consumers who holiday for this reason (e.g. low cost or easy access).

Previous guests

Identify and promote to those guests who have stayed before.

The marketing mix

Before the marketing mix decision is made, determine what purpose these marketing efforts are going to serve. Are they to: deepen the customer base, increase market share, increase revenue, reach new geographic markets or increase occupancy?

After these objectives are established, determine a date for accomplishing these objectives. The marketing mix allows the bed & breakfast to combine different marketing decision areas such as services, promotion and advertising, pricing and place, to construct an overall marketing programme.

Products and services

Use the product or service itself as a marketing resource. Having something unique provides motivation behind advertising.

TIP
Provide the service you advertise.

While the ideas mentioned under market strategy apply here, another option is to change or modify the service. Additional attention may be given to a product if it has changed colour, size or style, while a service may draw similar attention by modifying the services provided. Remember, sales and promotional opportunities are generated by product differentiation.

Promotion and advertising

With the marketing strategy and clear objectives outlined, use advertising to get the message out to the customers. Advertising can be through: directories such as *Yellow Pages* or *Golden Pages*, a press release, a newspaper, billboards and posters, B&B guidebooks, local tourism publications, direct mail and, very importantly, all forms of social media, e.g. Facebook, LinkedIn, Instagram and Google.

The internet is a relatively cheap way to promote your B&B both domestically and overseas, and should now be considered the centrepiece of your overall marketing strategy.

There are now several global reservation platforms on which you can list your B&B, the main ones being TripAdvisor, Airbnb, Windu, Stayz and Booking.com. The commissions you are asked to pay range from 3 per cent to 15 per cent of the booking value.

One reason to advertise is to highlight promotional activities. This will serve both to highlight your property and to offer added incentive for customer patronage. For example, you may wish to promote midweek two-nights-for-the-price-of-one offers, coupons or gift vouchers or special activities e.g. murder-mystery evenings.

The aim is to use the money allocated to advertising and promotion to try to reach the largest number of people. This may be accomplished by using several different methods of advertising. Be creative and implement ideas.

The following are some ideas that could help increase the response from your advertising material. Good-quality advertising can be costly, but very rewarding. The emphasis is on 'good'. It's also worth considering full-page advertisements (particularly if you are targeting the luxury market), but *after* your first year of profitable trade. It is not always appropriate to spend large sums of money in your first year, especially in expensive national travel magazines, as people don't tend to keep them, and you will have other priorities for your marketing budget.

> **TIP**
> Invite local tourist information staff to visit. Give them a complimentary night's stay so they can experience what you have to offer. This can effectively sell your B&B.

Always write the headline from your prospective guest's point of view not your own

People tend not to look at their products and services from the perspective of the people buying them. The sooner your prospective guests recognise themselves and their own wants and needs in the words you use in your headline, the faster they will respond.

Use the words 'You', 'New' and/or 'How to' in your headline

These are proven words that capture attention. Connect them to a benefit your prospective guests may want, and your response will increase.

Make your opening sentence continue what you were talking about in the headline

If in your headline you promised your prospective guest a relaxing stay in your bed & breakfast, then say something in your opening sentence about this to get them even more excited about staying with you.

Tell your whole story in miniature by the time the first paragraph is over

People have a very short attention span. Try to telescope your entire story down to a soundbite in writing. Think of how they do this on the TV news, where they give you the key points of an item and then say, 'More at nine.' Far more people will read your copy, and the results should produce bookings. Use the rest of your copy to retell your story in more detail.

Use specific, powerful and true testimonials

No matter how honest or persuasive you are, people usually won't believe everything when they first read your copy. They need to get to know you and trust you. That can take some time, but unfortunately you don't want to wait. You have to persuade them right now. They will be much more likely to believe other people when those people are singing your praises. Include testimonials to enhance your credibility.

TIP

Always have a book of photographs available for guests who may wish to familiarise themselves with the local area.

Edit your copy ruthlessly

If a word doesn't keep the reader reading by making your copy more interesting, or what you are selling more appealing, cut it out. Copywriting is the art of doing more with fewer words. Every word has to work really hard, and your copy has to be easy to read.

Marketing performance

After the marketing-mix decision is implemented, the next step is to evaluate performance. With a detailed list of your objectives, monitor how well the decisions are developing.

Evaluate objectives such as:

- *Market share.* Has the increased share been reached?
- *Revenue volume.* Was the increase attained?
- *Strategy.* Did the combinations of target markets and strategy work effectively? Which ones didn't?

You should also evaluate the following decisions:

- Did the advertising efforts reach target groups?
- Were promotions timely?
- Did customers respond to specials, coupons or other incentives?

Additionally, consider the following:

- Is your bed & breakfast doing all it can to satisfy the guest?
- Is it easy for customers to find what they want at a competitive price?
- If these objectives were not reached, what were the reasons?
- If they worked well, what elements were most effective?

By evaluating performance after decisions have been made, there is reference for future decision-making, based on past results. In addition, periodically assess customer feelings and opinions towards your bed & breakfast and how well your guests' needs are being satisfied. This can be done through surveys, customer comments cards or simply by asking them, 'How did you enjoy your stay?'

Assessing performance and asking for customer input brings around market research again. Your marketing plan is a continuous effort to identify and adapt to changes in markets, customer taste and the economy for the success of your bed & breakfast.

Public relations

All B&Bs have certain things in common: if nothing else you are all dealing with people who are away from their home. Understanding what bed & breakfasts have to offer, and the people who patronise them, will play an important part in your marketing approach.

You can quite safely say people frequent bed & breakfasts for:

- the personal, pampered feeling they offer;
- the safety and security offered by smaller establishments;
- the opportunity for closer interaction with local surroundings; and
- their suitability for short holiday breaks.

Taking these factors into account you could very well find that public relations could offer your bed & breakfast your cheapest and most effective form of promotion.

Media relations, where you try to influence journalists and producers of newspapers, magazines, radio shows and TV programmes to do a story on your bed & breakfast, at little or no cost, is likely to be the most relevant sector of the PR market. Editorial, as we call this coverage, has more credibility than paid advertising and gives an opportunity to cover more facts.

A *media kit* is the introduction, story, photographs and any other appropriate materials, such as brochures, which you send to the media. The most important component of this kit is the story, or the press release. Used well, a series of press releases can keep your establishment 'in the news'.

Look not only at promoting yourself, but also the attractions of your area, offering your bed & breakfast as the most convenient place to stay.

Press releases

The following are some rules to observe when preparing a press release.

- Write your story considering the questions, 'WHO? WHAT? WHY? WHEN? WHERE? and HOW?' This will help you to include all relevant information.
- You must remain focused on what your story is and ensure it appears different from all the other media kits that appear on journalists' desks daily. If it isn't clear to you, it won't be to them.
- Restrict your story to one A4-size page. Use your letterhead, as it contains your address and other contact details. Also include your contact name and phone number at the end of your story.
- Your press release must be typed with, at least 1.5 line spacing. Publisher, a Microsoft program, comes with a format specifically for

media releases.

- Make your story clear and concise, using simple language. Have a short and punchy title.
- Do not exaggerate: tell it like it is. Remember this may appear in print and you have to be able to deliver.
- Pay attention to details such as dates and times.
- Double-check your spelling. This attention to detail is seen as basic courtesy by journalists.

Targeting your story

If your emphasis is on food, naturally food sections of newspapers or gourmet magazines are where your story is best suited. If you offer unique scenery, try the travel section of a weekend paper. If you have gardens that have won awards, then the home or gardening section could be an opportunity.

Prior to writing your release, read the sections you are targeting carefully to understand what it is in each story that captured the imagination of the editor and made it topical.

Get to know your local papers, their deadlines and the names of staff you will be targeting. Being an active member of your community will enhance your chance of getting a media profile.

A week after posting your media kit follow it up with a phone call. Ask if the media kit has been received. If not, explain briefly what it is about and offer to send another copy. If they have seen it, ask them if they need more information and if they think the story is suitable.

Instead of a traditional media kit, you may consider offering journalists and their partners a first-hand experience of your bed & breakfast. A free night's accommodation is a cheap price to pay for a glowing report in a popular magazine or travel section of a newspaper. A journalist's visit will not necessarily provide you with fantastic copy or even an article, but 'freebies' or 'familiarisations' for journalists are part of the system, and positive word-of-mouth reports would always be to your advantage.

For best effect, limit the period of the offer so journalists are less likely to put it away and forget about you. Good editorial coverage may not make your business, but can provide the icing on the cake of your marketing plan. Well done, it is economical and effective.

Public relations are also about relations with your local community. Build up positive relationships with local clubs and business organisations, so you and your business become known and trusted by the locals. Public relations may also include sponsoring a fundraising event, horse race or local sports team, for example.

There are a number of books available on how to make public relations work for you.

The media unit of your regional tourism association can also provide information and support. You may wish to consider using a public relations consultancy for your initial promotion.

You advise the consultant of what you have in mind and your approximate budget, and they will come back to you with a proposal. The advantage of a good PR consultancy is that they already have the writing skills and media contacts to make the exercise effective, so your budget can be money well spent.

> **TIP**
> Think carefully, particularly on the choice of medium, before spending money on advertising.

How much marketing do you need?

Any expenses incurred in promoting your business can be set against any tax you might pay on your profits. However, this can be complicated when you are first embarking upon your venture. Consult your accountant before spending any money. What you should not do is decide that you need a certain type of advertisement just because that's what everyone else does. You must decide what is appropriate to your B&B at any given time. You should, however, have some idea about who it is you are trying to attract and how best to reach them.

A marketing plan and budget needs to be developed in conjunction with your business plan.

Bed & breakfast guides

Over the last few years many countries' B&B guides have closed down mainly because most people are travelling with their tablets/smartphones that enable them to very quickly search for B&Bs located in the areas they want to visit.

If, however, there are several bed & breakfast guides that you can list your property in then, when you are making your choice, you should look at the following:

- How many years has the guide been in existence?
- How many copies does the publisher print?
- How many copies do they actually sell or give away?
- Where is it for sale or distributed?
- How much is it sold for or is it free?
- How often and when does the guide come out?
- Do you like the method of presentation?
- Do they have a related website?
- How much does it cost?

Marketing plan

A marketing plan should outline your marketing goals for a twelve-month period and how you expect to achieve them through advertising, promotion, marketing and public relations. You should include the following elements: tourist information centres, direct mail campaigns (including newsletters), public relations (community and media activities), advertising, brochure stationery, business stationery, group promotions, websites, trade and tourism shows, and any other activity that will get your bed & breakfast noticed by the public.

Carefully consider any promotional or marketing schemes and opportunities offered to you by your local or regional tourism organisations. The benefits here can be considerable.

Your marketing plan will identify your target market and how you plan to reach it.

Do not forget your local community. Word of mouth is the best advertising for any business. Locals will continually be asked for their accommodation recommendations.

Join your local Chamber of Commerce, Rotary or Lions Club. Include membership fees, donations and sponsorships in your marketing plan budget.

Also allow for hidden costs such as photography, artwork design and production. A contingency of 12 per cent will allow for incidentals and price rises for the year.

> **TIP**
> Just because you have your B&B listed in a B&B guide does not mean you can sit back and wait for the phone to ring. There are many operators who have spent thousands on promoting their business in inappropriate journals with little success.

> **TIP**
> Remember the old adage 'you have to spend money to make money'. Doing things on the cheap is usually a waste of your hard-earned cash.

Social media

Social media should play an important role in your overall marketing strategy. The statistics emphasise this:

- Almost 50 per cent of the travel brands on Facebook found that their bookings increased due to social networking (Digital Visitor).
- 92 per cent of consumers say they trust earned media, such as social media, word of mouth and recommendations from friends and family, above all forms of advertising (Webbed Feet).
- 36 per cent of online travellers visit social network sites to influence destination selection (World Travel Market London).
- 87 per cent of those younger than thirty-four are using Facebook to solicit advice before making bookings (Stikky Media).
- 80 per cent of travellers are more likely to book a trip from a friend liking a page rather than responding to a traditional Facebook ad (Eye for Travel).
- Worldwide, there are over 1.5 billion active Facebook users, with 699 million people logging in daily (Zephoria).
- Twitter is one of the most heavily trafficked search engines in the world, serving over one billion queries per day (Stikky Media).
- Twitter has 500 million registered users whose posts amount to 175 million tweets per day (Stikky Media).
- TripAdvisor has a monthly visitor inflow of 57 million people, as well as a member base that exceeds 36 million (TripAdvisor).
- Social media is now a genuine marketing platform, with 93 per cent of marketers using social media to their advantage (Social Media B2B).
- Social media is one of the most successful ways to market your bed & breakfast, with more than 50 per cent of direct bookings coming from social media accounts (Frederic Gonzalo).
- 71 per cent of travel brands on Facebook found that they had better engagement and conversation with their customers (Digital Visitor).

If you don't know how to promote your B&B using all the available social media avenues offered, then engage someone who does.

Brochures

Your top marketing priorities will be; to ensure that you become involved with your tourist information centre, become part of any local tourist authority initiatives and create an effective brochure.

To enable you to ascertain what will attract your target market, look at your competitors' brochures. Consider what you like, the cost involved, and make it happen.

Remember that you can make a one-colour brochure be as effective as a four-colour brochure if you use the medium carefully. You must ensure your brochure is well written, easy to read, attractive and informative.

> **TIP**
> Don't think about putting your rates in your brochure. Print your brochure and have a computer-generated insert with rates. This will ensure you can use your brochure long after your rates have gone up, i.e. its so-called shelf-life can be extended indefinitely.

Newsletters

Newsletters are an effective way to communicate with your community and with past guests.

Microsoft Publisher has a number of options on template you can adapt for your bed & breakfast. These are a great way to create a positive presence in your community and reinforce all the elements of your marketing plan. These newsletters need not be expensive. You can design them on your computer, photocopy them or even email them to your mailing list.

If you include interesting topics and amusing text, they could be passed on to friends. You might want to have the occasional special offer to ascertain effectiveness.

Business stationery

Your business stationery should reflect the design of your brochures and the style of your B&B itself. You need to ensure that all of aspects of your promotions are part of one cohesive package.

Get a professional photographer to photograph your B&B. They may cost what is considered a lot of money, but it will be worth it and you'll have the photos forever.

The photos of your property can be used on your website, on social media, e.g. Facebook, in your brochures and in your advertisements.

TIP

Have your letterhead printed on A5 as well as A4 paper as you are often only sending out short notes.

14 The Fundamentals of Business

No matter what the financial or personal expectations for your new venture, it is a business and you need to treat it with the gravity it deserves. You will find it impossible to achieve the results you want without a blueprint on how you plan to get there.

In this chapter, we aim to give you all the advice you need to get you started in your venture.

Find the workbook we talked about in the first chapter and write down your answers to the following questions:

Do I have any business experience? Write down how you believe you can use this experience in your new business.

Do I have any other experiences I can draw on? How do I believe they will help me?

Have I spoken to an accountant or financial advisor?

Have I contacted my national tourism office or local tourism organisation to get information on my country's tourism statistics?

Have I spoken to my national or regional bed & breakfast association?

Have I determined the financial goals I have for the business?

Have I discussed with my financial advisor the effect that turning my house into a business will have on my financial affairs? If applicable, have you registered for VAT/GST? Talk to your financial advisor for more information.

Have I looked at various tourism industry publications?

Have I sought the opinions of potential customers and suppliers?

Have I worked out a financial plan to supplement my income while I build my business?

> **TIP**
> Make a practical, concrete business plan, with seven parts implementation for every one part strategy.

Financing

In the first year of your new enterprise you should try and finance your venture yourself. However, if additional funding is necessary you need to ensure you contact your small-business association, your bank or credit union, or a financial advisor. Remember, all start-up businesses need seed capital and a B&B is not an exception.

Choosing a legal structure

Choosing the legal structure within which your business will trade is one of the first decisions you will need to make. You must discuss the best options for you with your solicitor and financial advisor.

To help arm you for the meeting, a synopsis of your options is provided below. You must not make your final decision based on this, as each business's financial position is different and only your solicitor and your financial advisor have the tools to decide which structure best suits your situation.

It is worth noting at this point that you must be honest with your financial advisor and solicitor about your financial position. They will make the decisions regarding your financial affairs based on the information you give them. If you withhold information it will only be to your financial detriment.

Sole trader

The main advantage of being a sole trader is that you are your own boss. The profits are all yours, but so are the losses. You make all the decisions relating to the business yourself – something that can be both a positive and a negative. Tax breaks are usually not as generous. The main disadvantage is that you are personally liable for any business debts, which could put your personal assets at risk.

Partnership

A partnership requires two or more people. It has the advantage of pooling resources: financial, experience, brains. It also disperses the risk. Commonly cited disadvantages are disagreements over decision-making and unequal distribution of work. A partnership agreement is an essential tool that will clarify from the outset the responsibilities of each partner. The time spent working this out at the beginning of the partnership minimises possible disagreements later. Your solicitor can help you draw up this agreement.

Company

A company is a separate entity from its shareholders and as such continues to exist when members change. It is created by incorporation under the corporation law. The company structure allows you to separate your personal activities from your business activities. Tax advantages are good but you may still incur personal liability for the company.

Trusts

This is definitely a decision for your financial advisor. Trusts are administered by the trustee for the benefit of the beneficiaries of the trust. There are a few different types of trusts and your financial advisor will best be able to advise you of their benefits.

Business names

Be sure to register your business name, for example Hannan House, to protect your investment.

So, what is a 'business name'? It is a name used by any person, partnership, company or trust for running a business, unless it is the same as their own name. It is advisable to consult a solicitor before using a business name.

Ideally, you choose three names (in order of preference) that you would like to have, then search online for the name of the organisation that registers business names to see if any other business is already using your preferred choice. If some are, then try your second choice and so on until you can register a name that no one else is using.

Setting your room rate

Having decided what needs to be done to get your house ready for bed & breakfast, you are probably wondering, when you see that mental picture of the property already finished, what your room rate should be in the first operating year. We suggest that you take a calculated guess. Let us assume, for the sake of this exercise, that your guess is £/€/$90 per night per room.

Look up a B&B guide or search engine and find two properties that already charge £/€/$90 per night and book yourself in. Be sure that the two properties are located in a similar environment, but not necessarily in the same locality, as yours. For example, if your property is a coastal one, then find two others that are also located on the coast. You only need one night in each property.

On checking in, tell the host that you are shortly opening a bed & breakfast and that you would be grateful if they could share their experiences with you. Most B&B operators are happy to oblige.

While there, take the opportunity to check the level of hosting and facilities offered for £/€/$90 per night. Have a quick look in the guest book and note what comments previous guests have made. You may find that one out of every three remarks relate directly to the intrinsic beauty of the gardens. These comments may be the reason why the B&B is so popular.

After you have stayed in the two selected B&B properties, revisit your own mental picture of your finished B&B and you might find that what you are going to offer could attract a room rate of £/$/€100 per night or, conversely, £/€/$80 per night. In this way, you are going to make a more informed decision.

Determining pricing levels and pricing policies is the major factor affecting revenue. Factors such as demand, the market price and customer responsiveness to price changes influence the price levels. Other factors such as a convenient location or a more personalised service may allow a bed & breakfast to charge a higher room rate.

In some countries, there is a regulation in place that requires properties with more than four guestrooms to display the minimum and maximum room rates in a prominent place.

> **TIP**
> Don't underestimate the cost of food when setting your room rate. If you provide a gourmet breakfast, you need to make money out of it.

Market mix

Now we get to the fun part. Let us assume that your proposed room rate is £/€/$60 per night and that you have three guestrooms, all with their own en-suites and priced the same.

Now, we assume that in the first operating year your occupancy rate is targeted at 40 per cent. That means we have approximately 21 weeks of projected bookings, which represents 146 days x 3 guestrooms = 438 room nights. If every booking was worth £/€/$60 then the annual turnover would be £/€/$26,280.

But will all of your bookings be direct? You see we need to now consider the 'market mix': your bookings may come from different sources that attract different levels of pricing. In the table shown, we list the various booking sources and room rates the same could attract.

Booking Source	Room Nights Sold (No.)	Percentage Share (%)	Room Rate Charged (£/€/$)	Receipts (£/€/$)
Direct	252	60	60	15,120
Off-peak	44	11	55	2420
Corporate	44	10	50	2200
Internet	76	14	45	3420
Tour operator	22	5	50	1100
Total	**438**	**100**	**55 = Ave. Room Rate**	**24,260**

In this example, actual receipts show that the average room rate was £/€/$55 per night, not £/€/$60 as first thought. This demonstrates the effect of market mix. Ideally, you do some research in order to gauge where your bookings are likely to originate and budget accordingly.

If you find that the vast majority of bookings originate from sources that attract a low room rate, then you may wish to adjust your marketing strategy and in turn your projected profit and loss figures. Don't forget seasonality factors.

Taxation and the B&B

The following does not apply in some countries, but usually there is a range of business tax regulations governing the running of a bed & breakfast. Sometimes, rules governing business rate payments by guest-accommodation establishments have been in place for some years, but have been applied more rigorously in recent times and have become a significant factor in many local economies.

So what are business rates?

Business rates are a national tax on the occupation of non-domestic property paid to, and administered by, central government although the revenue is used to provide local services. With a few specific exceptions, each non-domestic property has a rateable value, which is based on the market rent it would be expected to command.

In some places, a B&B property is deemed domestic and therefore subject to normal council tax, rather than business rates, if:

- you intend not to provide short-stay accommodation for more than six people at any one time in the coming year; or
- the property is your sole residence and the bed & breakfast use is subsidiary to the private use.

As a rough guide, if half or more of the whole house (not just bedrooms) is devoted to B&B guests at any one time, then the property is likely to be business rated.

We suggest strongly that you consult with your accountant or tax agent as to your true position, and suggest you check out the ruling on the above with your national/state tax office. Your accountant can also advise you.

Capital gains tax

When you sell a property you may have to pay capital gains tax (CGT) – not on the whole amount you sell it for, but on the gain you make in selling it. However, there are various tax reliefs available and to that end we suggest you seek advice from your accountant.

VAT/GST

With VAT/GST, as applicable, there is much your business will need to do to ensure it is compliant. The other concern for you regarding taxation is that you are turning, in most cases, your family home into a business. *You will need very good taxation advice prior to taking in your first guest.* Make this a top priority: talk to your accountant.

Computer literacy

Computers have become an important factor in our daily lives. Like it or not, they are ubiquitous. Everywhere we go there seems to be a computer involved, be it when banking, visiting a doctor or dentist and at the checkout counters of any supermarket or department store. Our car engines are controlled by them and many of our mobile phones are now, in fact, mobile computers hosting cut-down operating systems.

Schoolchildren are taught to use computers as a crucial element of their education; typewriters are now something out of a bygone era. We now depend on these machines to operate a vast range of software programs that enable us to more effectively run our businesses, manage our calendars and communicate with family and friends around the globe.

Although the clear majority of households own computers, for many they remain mysterious and perhaps even threatening. This needn't be so, for it is important that all of society accepts the challenge and becomes computer literate. Not to do so can inhibit one from having one's say in the knowledge-based information era in which we all now live.

Throughout the world, there are many local learning faculties or tertiary colleges that run introductory computer courses at very competitive rates. If you have not already done so, you should enrol in one now. There are also businesses and individuals who offer in-home training to assist with the transition to using computers. The longer you leave becoming technologically literate, the more difficult it is going to be.

Purchasing a computer

Purchase the best model you can afford. It's true that computers become cheaper every day and the computer you buy today will be outdated, if not tomorrow, in around eighteen months. However, if you buy the best you can afford now it is likely to be around for longer, even as technology surpasses it. It is not a case of waiting until the upgrading of computers stops. That is not going to happen any time soon and it would be a false economy to purchase one with this in mind. The bottom line is that it is almost impossible to do business today without the use of a computer.

Before making a purchase determine your primary needs. Desktop machines offer greater performance at a lower price, but powerful laptops are becoming ever cheaper and offer considerable flexibility for travel.

Pay particular attention to the warranty terms applicable to the machine and do take the advice of a knowledgeable specialist you trust.

The internet and your website

Which brings us to the internet. During the past forty years very few people (other than perhaps the Amish and some neo-Luddites) would have considered doing business without having access to a telephone, and during the last twenty years most businesses would consider it essential to have a fax machine. For most businesses today, the internet is already an essential tool; indeed, it is difficult to think of an area of business to which it doesn't already extend.

Smartphones have been with us long enough for people to consider them a natural extension of communication using the voice and text. A computer/smartphone, with connection to the internet, has the capability to extend or expand all areas of audio, visual and written communication. Remember the difference between a taxi and Uber, and a hotel and a B&B, is partly communication.

A computer can be used as an alternative to the traditional phone (even adding video through webcam) for communication and, in the form of email, replace or supplement the use of the fax machine. It can be used to replace printed photographs and video cassettes with live audio/visual connections. This area of communications is just the tip of the iceberg. The internet is revolutionising almost every aspect of human endeavour.

Areas affected include advertising, entertainment, education, reference material and shopping. The list goes on and on. One of the prime areas it has revolutionised is travel. A traveller may quickly map out her trip, choosing locations and accommodation after perusing photos or videos, reading online travel magazines or peer reviews, and ultimately book and pay for car hire, flights and rooms all from the comfort of her living room.

Accessing the web is an integral part of our existence, so a vast number of people use the internet when booking accommodation.

Still, when it comes to the internet, a significant number of people are at the same stage as a child picking up a telephone receiver for the first time to say 'Hello.' It's a steep learning curve and one that a lot of us think we would rather not climb. But we have reached a critical juncture. The internet is no longer just one of many tools that can help us 'thrive' in business, but is becoming a necessary instrument required to 'survive' in business.

Creating a website

Determine early on the level of involvement you intend to have in creating your site. Are you going to design and create it yourself, or will you pay a professional to create it for you? In either case, the best place to begin is to spend time studying the web, looking at as many sites in the B&B industry as possible, and determining what works and what doesn't. When you see a site you like that someone else has created, be sure to note the address and give it to your web designer.

If you intend to create the site yourself, you may save pages that you like so that you can examine the HTML and see how it was done. You can then adapt the same for your own requirements. Buy or download for free a WYSIWYG editor, such as Adobe Dreamweaver or Microsoft Expression Web, as they have useful tutorials and samples and access to good technical support.

Before you can launch a website, you will need to purchase and register a domain name. The domain name is the name of your site and will cost you a recurring annual fee with the registrar. You also need to choose a web hosting company that will host your website on their servers. Get as much advice and assistance as you require in these early stages. A strong, memorable domain name is crucial, so be careful in your choice.

On the web, there are many sites that provide tutorials and explanations of every aspect of website design and implementation. Scores of quality teach-yourself books exist in this arena; read reviews of books online to find the best one for you. Spend time on your site and experiment. Create a style. Keep it simple and start small as you can always add more detail and give it more impact later on.

Publish and announce your site to friends, search engines and directories, but most of all refine the site and widen your goals and learning experiences. It may well be that the best option is to hook onto a community website or source local directories to appear on. Seek local advice, as with every aspect of your B&B business.

TIP
We are in the Knowledge & Communication era!

Your web design must reflect your goals and, once those have been identified and an agreed structure is in place, then the site design and construction can commence.

This process is very different from designing a newspaper advertisement, which can remain static, as it needs to be maintained and updated at regular intervals.

Be sure that you clearly determine the goals of your bed & breakfast site. Is the goal to provide a service, list your property or supply some other service such as an index or registry? Visitors to your site will be looking for the listed material: *Who are the hosts? What facilities do you offer? What are your room rates? How can you be contacted? Why should I stay at your B&B instead of someone else's? Can I book directly from the site? What is the availability like on my required dates?*

Make sure that your website is easy to navigate. This is an incredibly important but often overlooked aspect of web design. At least 35 per cent of visitors will arrive on your homepage first, with most hits directly fed from a search result, before they then click on to a secondary page on your site. Thus, site navigation is crucial and must be clear, user-friendly and consistent across your website. Have navigation buttons or text with informative descriptions that enable the visitor to know where they are going and what to expect. Your homepage should be simple, striking and memorable. Like a good magazine cover, it should contain strong visual imagery, a clear 'headline' and just enough information to encourage a visitor to read more.

Your homepage might list the features of your bed & breakfast site so be sure it's interesting enough to lead to a return visit. Visual aids, particularly for accommodation, are very important. Have a good photographer take high-quality photos of your establishment.

A well-designed website can become an effective marketing and selling tool for your bed & breakfast. If you don't feel up to the challenge of designing it yourself there is an abundance of web designers who will design one for you for fees ranging from the very high to the very low.

But beware, like everything else, your website must have a professional appearance if you're not going to waste your money. Be careful whom you choose to set up your site. There are charlatans who will charge thousands for a service that shouldn't cost more than a few hundred. Ask to see examples of their work and the 'hits' they are attracting (the number of people who look at the sites and the average time spent on it). In the future, it could well become your major instrument for generating bookings.

Again, research will pay dividends. Once your website is up and running you will need to make sure people can find it.

Maximising your web presence

Submitting your website to the numerous search engines is the first step to making an appearance in the list of properties displayed in a web search. With more and more businesses striving to gain a visible online presence, the market is becoming flooded. In real terms, this means it is becoming increasingly hard to get your business listed among the top few for contextual searches. It is now commonplace for businesses to pay good money to achieve a high rank in appropriate search results – an endeavour known as Search Engine Optimisation (SEO). In 2016, it was estimated that 88 per cent of companies will pay to advertise on Google, 39 per cent on Yahoo and 36 per cent on Bing.

Google searches generate the greatest part of web traffic and, when it comes to SEO, the related products Google AdSense and Google Analytics are the most popular.

If managing your own web presence is beyond your resources, there are many businesses that specialise in boosting search rankings.

If you are serious about increasing the number of visitors to your site, it is important that you analyse your existing web traffic. Answering the following questions will allow you to refine your meta-tags (keywords embedded in the HTML code of your site), and to determine areas of strength and weakness:

- *Which search engines are feeding me the most visitors?*
- *From which countries do I get the most traffic?*
- *Which of my pages are the most popular?*
- *Are there any particular sites that commonly send me traffic?*
- *What search phrases or keywords are used most frequently?*

Outside the world of search engines, the recent popularity of social networking sites such as Facebook and Twitter has prompted a rethink of traditional web advertising. Facebook is now the UK's second most popular site after Google. It should come as no surprise, then, that the majority of businesses are currently adopting social media marketing (SMM) as an additional advertising avenue.

It is thought that, in 2018, at least 84 per cent of businesses will market themselves on Twitter, making it the most widely adopted social media for marketing, just ahead of Facebook with 81 per cent.

Paid search marketing should not be overlooked as an option to help deepen your presence on the internet. Do be sure to set established measures of success to judge your return on income, such as analysing the number of clicks or visitors, number of phone enquiries, etc.

Choosing an internet provider

If you are not yet connected to the internet, be sure to shop around for the deal that matches your needs. There are a number of technologies available for connecting to the web, from dial-up (inexpensive, but slow), to a range of much faster broadband offerings including cable, DSL (digital subscriber line), wireless broadband and satellite. DSL is the most popular and is a cost-effective technology in the UK, with almost absolute geographic coverage. Before making a purchase, we suggest you firstly determine what you are likely to use the web for. If you want to do more than simple emailing or web browsing, you will need a plan with faster speeds and a higher download limit. If you start out with a modest speed and data limit, you should be able to alter the terms of your arrangement with your chosen service provider as need arises. Ask potential providers about any available package deals, as you may save money by bundling your internet connection with your telephone or television services.

SWOT analysis

SWOT is simply a shorthand description of the exercise where you look at the **S**trengths and **W**eaknesses of your own business, and the **O**pportunities and **T**hreats it is facing in the marketplace.

Your SWOT analysis is a two-stage exercise. In stage one, you look at your business and ask, *How do my clients [that is, actual and potential] see my business in relation to my competition?* plus *What is important to them and why?* and *What are the main points on which they will focus?*

Make a list of these key points and then analyse each one to decide if your clients would see each individual point as either:

- a strength that your business has and your competition does not; or
- a weakness that needs to be addressed.

Typical key points you might consider are:

Reputation	value for money, repeat clients, outstanding meals
Rating	as per tourism authority or bed & breakfast association
Managers & staff	friendly, efficient, experienced, trained, client-focused, receptive
Location	proximity to attractions, isolated, easily found, views
Facilities	secure parking, dining room, restaurant, grounds, pools, equipment, e-commerce
Décor & rooms	style, room size, presentation, themes
Promotion	coverage, effectiveness, website, association membership, signage
Price	relative to target market

Profitability	good or bad, high or low?
Rooms	size, maintenance, inclusions, access
Meals	quality, quantity, uniqueness, flexibility, use of local produce

Involve your staff in creating this list and don't exclude any points simply because 'Everyone knows that!' What is obvious to you could turn out to be a critical factor that none of your competitors have discovered.

Once you have completed your list of strengths and weaknesses, create two short lists of, for example, six key strengths and six key weaknesses.

In stage two of your SWOT analysis, you should look at your business again, but with a different focus. Instead of looking at the internal factors of your business over which you have control, look this time at the industry and identify external factors that will affect or influence your future operations. As you identify each factor, ask, *What's in it for me?* and decide whether these factors provide you with either an opportunity for growth and profitability, or a threat to your existence or profitability.

Stand back and think 'outside the box'. Look for changes in the marketplace, e.g. in regulations, in competitors and their activities, in economic development, technology, etc. Be aware of emerging trends in the B&B industry overseas and try to forecast the possible impact on your market.

Some examples of key points are:

Competition	development activity, closures, new competition, change of ownership, upgrades
Legislation	new requirements for B&Bs, occupational health & safety changes, award rate increases, taxation changes, insurance
Technology	e-commerce, reservation and billing software
Economic factors	recession, industry moves, industrial disputes, changes in demand
Industry promotions	new tourism bodies and regional promotions
Other	local news (good/bad), local and special events, i.e. conferences

Again, involve your staff in creating and analysing these points, and create a short list of opportunities and threats to focus your thinking and planning.

From this SWOT analysis you have:

- Identified your key strengths – which you want to protect and promote.
- Identified your key weaknesses – which you want to address and fix.
- Identified your opportunities in the marketplace – which you would like to exploit.
- Identified the potential and actual threats – to the profitability and survival of your business, which must be addressed.

> **TIP**
> If you are always putting out fires then build a sprinkler system. You can lose the forest by paying too much attention to the trees.

The issues identified in the SWOT analysis should be addressed and incorporated into your business plan.

You should now know where you are.

The next stage in the planning process is to look at the future and decide:

- where you want to be (your objectives);
- how to get there (your strategies); and
- proof of your progress (your milestones).

> **TIP**
> Start your planning process by defining exactly what you want – that is, set your objectives.

Your future

Some people actually do make money in spite of themselves, but most successful people plan for success.

Objectives

Objectives are concise and measurable statements that outline what you want to achieve within a given time span. The direction and focus of your business objectives will come from key areas, namely:

- your mission statement;
- your personal objectives;
- your current position analysis; and
- your SWOT analysis.

Your mission statement should explain why your business exists, what it does and what it hopes to achieve.

It is the final point – what it hopes to achieve – that is critical in setting your objectives. For example, the emphasis may be on the desire 'To maintain our ranking in the nation's list of top-twenty most romantic venues'. This statement sets the focus on the style and theme of operation and the type of guests to be targeted, the promotion to be undertaken, and the quality of the accommodation and surroundings that must be maintained.

> **TIP**
>
> As an owner of a business, it is important to remember that your business is only a means of achieving what you want in your private life.

In simple terms, your private life must take precedence over your business life – even though, in practice, the reverse seems to happen more often than not. Your personal objectives could well impact on your business objectives by limiting your business hours, influencing your investment decisions, balancing family and guests' usage of your facilities, etc.

Your current position analysis will obviously give you a base for setting your business objectives, and your SWOT analysis will give you focus.

The mechanics of setting objectives are not difficult. Instead of thinking of your business as a whole, try breaking it down (in your mind) into a few key areas. Pick a date in the future, say six months, twelve months or even three years ahead, and visualise how you perceive that key area at that time.

To work through an example, start by selecting your key areas, for example:

Your operation

- operational, e.g. facilities, systems;
- management and staff;
- marketing, e.g. promotions, offers, services; and
- finance and funding results, e.g. profitability, return on investment, occupancy, industry ratings, etc.

Then (after consulting your mission statement, your current situation analysis and the key points in your SWOT analysis) write down what you want to achieve.

Examples could be:

- By ../../....
- To have new computerised booking and billing systems
- To increase total occupancy by x per cent
- To upgrade our industry rating to say four stars
- To conduct a six-week study tour of B&Bs in a specific area
- To increase gross takings to an annual level of x
- To lift net profit from the existing x per cent to y per cent
- To establish a corporate clientele of at least 50 per cent of total monthly sales

While it is vital that you include a completion date in your objectives, remember that you don't have to achieve all your results immediately. Some objectives will require a longer time frame; for short-, medium- and long-term objectives the time periods might be up to six months, six months to two years, and two to five years.

Also, don't try to be too ambitious. Pick out the objectives you consider to be most critical to your operation – say three to four objectives from each key area, e.g. operational, staff, marketing and financial.

> **TIP**
> The next step is to make your objectives happen by developing your strategic plans.

Strategies for success

A strategy, in lay terms, is simply a planned course of action designed to achieve a given objective. The easiest way to develop a strategy is to look at your objective, ask the basic question *How are we going to do that?* and start brainstorming.

Involve your partner/s and your team and don't dismiss any ideas in the initial stage as 'no use', 'too hard' or 'can't be done'. It is often the 'way-out' or 'stupid' ideas that breed genius and results.

Once you have all the ideas on paper, then analyse them and come up with a summary of your proposed course of action. As an example, let us assume that your analysis of your current position has shown your major client segment to be from the budget market, and despite the high quality of your offerings, you are catering for few of the more affluent guests. Furthermore, despite your proximity to a business area, you have no corporate clientele. Just to make the situation worse, your SWOT analysis also reveals that the three nearby establishments are displaying 'no vacancy' signs on a continuous basis.

On the strength of this information, you and your team can see an opening in the corporate market, which can command a better room rate, midweek occupancy and a different type of guest. You and your team develop an objective: 'To develop a corporate clientele of at least 50 per cent of our average monthly bookings within the next twelve months.'

To achieve this objective, the strategies you develop could be summarised along the lines of: 'To establish the accommodation needs and preferences of corporate clients and use the results of this research to change our image, our offerings and our promotional activities and effectiveness.'

From this strategy statement, it is obvious that much has to be done before the objective can be achieved. A list of jobs, or action steps, should be created and responsibility should be allocated for their completion. In creating this list, allocate completion times to each action step and also try to estimate the cost of each step.

Such a list could look like this:

Action Step Research	Responsibility	Due Date	Cost £/€/$
List of potential corporate clients	SW	18/7/19	N/A
Needs audit of clients	SW	18/7/19	N/A
Establish origin of clients	SW	18/7/19	N/A
Conduct own promotional audit	SH		N/A
Create a business event diary for next 12 mths	SH	18/7/19	N/A
Promotion			
Design and develop new publicity folder	ADS	20/8/19	1500
Print and distribute new folders	ADS	27/8/19	2500
Inclusion in community website	RDA	20/8/19	400
Implement changes suggested from own promotional audit	ADS	Set programme	TBA
Premises upgrade			
Provide work centres in each room	CD	1 month	800 each
Install ADSN facility	CD	24/7/19	500,
			+130/mth

Selling activity			
Join Chamber of Commerce	SW	Now	250
Join Rotary	SW	Now	300
Visit 10 potential clients per week	All	Ongoing	N/A
Place follow-up call with all guests within 2 weeks to obtain feedback & solicit referrals	JA	Ongoing	N/A
Attend all major events on business calendar	All	Ongoing	TBA
Price policy			
Decide on new policy & discount offers where applicable	All	Now	N/A
Staff			
Create new roster to service new client needs	BA	13/9/19	Nil
Reports			
Generate monthly reports on corporate clients' average billing, repeat clients, etc	SW	Monthly	Nil

As you can see, this example is not exhaustive – but it goes a long way towards organising a plan of action to achieve the objective of attracting corporate clients. It is all very well to have such a plan, but what can you do to make it work?

Milestones

Milestones, as the name implies, are physical guides to advise you of your location and progress along your journey. In the implementation of your business plan, milestones serve the same purpose, i.e. to advise you of your progress with your action steps. They are proof that the action steps you have identified and allocated have actually been completed. Let us return to the action steps discussed above. The milestones for these action steps could be simply:

- Client list created
- Customer survey completed
- Analysis mechanism established

- Business diary created
- Promotional brochure printed
- Website complete
- Connection of high-speed data access for PC

You need to plan to achieve each of your objectives by:

1. stating your objective in writing;
2. summarising your strategies;
3. listing your action steps;
4. identifying the milestone required.

Due to the fact that each strategy can have a large number of action steps, your worksheet should be presented in two pages to accommodate the listing of all steps and milestones.

TIP
A good business plan is a practical one. It must have realistic goals that can be implemented. It will guide decisions.

15 A Hypothetical Business Plan for B&B Operators

The following pages set out a suggested format that can be used when developing your own business plan.

Disclaimer: this is a hypothetical study and should be used for information only. If you have any specific business concerns please consult appropriate professional advisors. No liability can be accepted for loss or expense incurred as a result of relying on particular circumstances or statements made in this study.

Business Plan for Berkley Cottage, 2018–2019

Property Owner : Mr A. Brownley
Address
Email Address
Phone No.
Mobile No.

Contents

3

Contact Information

Mr A. Brownley
Address
Email
Phone No.
Mobile No.

Professional Support

Accountant – name, address
Solicitor – name, address
Banker – name, bank, branch
Mentor – name, address
Tourist office – contact name and address
Insurance company – name

4

Executive Summary

This business plan is developed for Berkley Cottage, a three-guestroom bed & breakfast.

The property is run-down and requires substantial refurbishment and adjustment to cater for the discerning guest who is looking to stay in a four-star bed & breakfast.

I purchased this property for £€$276,000 and have allowed for a further £€$80,000, which I have to pay for the cost of the refurbishment. I have set in place a timeline for completion of nine months, which means I aim to open for business late spring 2018.

My wife and I will do most of the work ourselves thus keeping our costs down, but we will employ tradesmen who have skills that we don't have.

Over the years we have stayed in many bed & breakfasts and have a good idea what facilities work and what doesn't work regarding property layout and guest creature comforts.

We have an accountant and solicitor who have worked with us in the past, and we have identified top tradesmen to be involved in the renovations.

Our property is in a street off the main road and is perfectly located for popular tourist walks and close to substantial shopping areas.

Both my wife and I have worked in the hospitality industry for a total of twenty years and subsequently have had a lot of exposure to the accommodation sector.

As I will continue working, my wife will be running the bed & breakfast, with me helping out with the administration and the manual tasks during the weekends. We will need to take out a small business loan of £€$2500 as initial seed capital to get the business off the ground.

Our goal at the beginning of our second year of operation is to achieve 60 per cent occupancy with a room rate of £€$70 per night that would generate revenue of £€$45,990 p.a.

5

We will have our website up and running at least three months before we open the doors as a bed & breakfast, with forward bookings in place from day one.

Mission Statement

'To provide an ambient, romantic experience for dreamers everywhere.'

Current Situation

We take possession of our property in July 2018 and subsequently have arranged for our renovation/refurbishment to commence within seven days of moving in.

As the centrepiece of our marketing strategy is our website, we will be briefing the web designer of the requirements to meet our bed & breakfast expectations with the aim of attracting bookings from day one of opening.

Market research indicates that our area is very popular with visitors who are seeking family history and those who take a keen interest in shopping for fashion items. It is these markets that we are going to target with the demographics being professional couples.

Business overview

Our trading name is Berkley Cottage. We will operate as a partnership. We are in constant contact with our local tourism office, which is providing us with meaningful tourist patterns including seasonal ones. We will be registering our partnership details with the appropriate authorities as instructed by our accountant.

The style of our property is Georgian. It will have three guestrooms with en-suites attached. Our guests will be able to access private living areas that have dining tables, lounge, TV and music facilities.

Our experience in hospitality along with our people skills will bode well when dealing with guests. Another factor that works in our favour is that our financial situation enables us to only have a small mortgage and, as I will be working, that means that we are not under financial pressure.

My wife will be running the bed & breakfast.

7

Organisational structure

In the first instance, we will refurbish the property to our required bed & breakfast standard. We both have had extensive experience in renovating properties as we have completed three projects. We have identified the tradesmen whom we wish to work with and will keeping a tight rein on expenses.

As already mentioned, my wife will be running the bed & breakfast with myself in charge of budgeting and manual tasks that are needed from time to time. My sister-in-law is on hand to help run the property in the event of illness or other reasons like having a holiday ourselves.

Market outline

Our area's share of the regional tourist pound is very good with visitor arrivals evenly spaced over the spring and summer periods. The market we are targeting is professional couples that are either from overseas or the UK. Current market share as it applies to our area is 75 per cent inbound and the remainder being from the UK, in particular England and Wales.

Our local tourism office keeps us up to date regarding major events and tourist patterns that might change every so often.

Competition

Most other bed & breakfast operators in the area are targeting the family market so there shouldn't be too much competition. Their guests share the bathroom due to the way in which the properties are set out, i.e. family guestrooms do not have separate en-suites.

8

SWOT analysis

Our strengths are:

- Financially strong in that we only need a small mortgage and I will be earning income that will complement the income generated from the bed & breakfast.
- We will have a unique bed & breakfast due to the fact that our property is being designed to suit our target market.
- Our website will reflect the bed & breakfast's high points including its close vicinity to local tourist attractions and high-end shops.
- We will be competitive with our room rates, therefore ensuring value for money.

Our weaknesses are:

- We are new to the business of running a bed & breakfast, and will have to work hard to get our share of the accommodation income.
- We have never been in business for ourselves before.
- It will take time to get overall business from word-of-mouth recommendations.

Our opportunities are:

- We are well positioned to attract professional couples who are in the area for work reasons as we are close to the commerce area of our town.
- The local tourism office keeps the accommodation sector abreast of coming events in order to attract visitors to our area.

Our threats are:

- A change in City Council regulations that will affect bed & breakfasts.
- Changing traffic patterns that divert drivers to outer areas outside of the town limits.
- Illness that affects our ability to work.

9

Objectives, Strategies and Milestones

Key objectives

The direction and focus of our business objectives will come from key areas, namely:

- our mission statement;
- personal objectives;
- current position analysis; and
- SWOT analysis.

The mission statement – is important to us as it explains why our bed & breakfast exists and what we hope to achieve. This statement sets the focus on the style and theme of operation and the type of guests (professional couples) to be targeted.

Personal objectives – one of which is the premise we are working from, that is: our business is only a means of achieving what we want in our private lives. To be successful in business and content in what we do are important steps towards a fulfilling life.

Our current position analysis – is the basis for setting our business objectives and our SWOT analysis. Our aim is to have the following in place by April 2018:

- computerised booking and billing system;
- occupancy levels reached 60 per cent and property graded;
- gross takings achieved in the first year of £€$22,995, annual income;
- to establish an inbound clientele of 60 per cent of total monthly sales.

The SWOT Analysis – is a must for it enables people to better see their true private and commercial position.

Strategies for success

- A good business plan in place that is our working document.
- Property refurbishment completed.
- A marketing strategy whose centrepiece is a well-put-together website in place.
- Using our local tourism association tourism data as a basis of our market research is vital, for following trends as they relate to both our market and locality is important. 'Think globally and act locally.'

Milestones

Below are the Milestones that we will expedite.

Action Step	Responsibility	Due Date
Research	AB	Ongoing
List of potential clients	AB	18/2
Establish origin of clients	AB	18/2
Conduct own promotional audit	JB	Open
Create a business event diary for next 12 mths	JB	18/3
Promotion	AB	Open
Design and develop new publicity folder	CS	20/4
Print and distribute new folders	CS	27/4
Inclusion in community website	RD	20/3
Website up and running	AB	14/2
Visit 10 potential clients per week	All	Ongoing
Attend all major events on business calendar	All	Ongoing
Decide on new policy & discount offers where applicable	All	Now
Reports	All	1/3

11

Forecasts

These include sales and income expenditure, and cash-flow patterns as follows:

Sales

Effectively sales commence mid-spring with an inbound guest occupancy averaging 33 per cent during the first three months and building up to 58 per cent in the next three. Our room rate is fixed for the first year at £70 per night.

Because we will have our website up and running three months prior to opening our doors as a bed & breakfast, planned occupancy levels should be maintained.

Visitor arrivals traditionally start coming into the immediate area in early spring with a substantial build-up of inbound tourists during the summer months.

Forecasting Occupancy Rates

Item	Apr	May	Jun	Jul	Aug	Sep
Professional couples	90%	90%	90%	100%	100%	100%
Inbound visitors	30%	30%	40%	50%	65%	60%
Domestic visitors	15%	15%	15%	15%	15%	10%
Total	45%	45%	55%	65%	75%	70%

Income and expenditure

The formula I have used to measure the profitability expenditure of our bed & breakfast is:

Sales income minus Direct Costs equals Gross Profit

Gross Profit minus Operating Costs equals Net Profit before tax and personal drawings

12

Forecasting Worksheet (6 months): Occupancy Levels against Room Rates

Item	Apr	May	Jun	Jul	Aug	Sep	Total
Inbound visitors	30%	30%	40%	50%	65%	60%	
3 guestrooms Rate							
££$70 per night each	1638	1638	2184	2730	3549	3276	15,015
Domestic Visitors	15%	15%	15%	15%	15%	10%	
Room rate ££$60 p/night	819	819	819	819	819	546	4641
Total	2457	2457	3003	3549	4368	3822	19,656

All operating costs are paid from my Gross Profit. Experience in the bed and breakfast industry shows that Direct Costs should be no more than 25% of revenue if you do most of the cleaning and domestic chores yourself.

13

Forecasting Worksheet: Forecast Profit for Period Ending 30/09/2018

Item	Apr	May	Jun	Jul	Aug	Sep	Total
Sales income – £/€/$	2457	2457	3003	3549	4368	3822	19,656
Cost of goods sold, e.g. food & provisions	719	719	878	1038	1278	1117	5749
Gross profit	1738	1738	2125	2511	3090	2705	13,907
LESS							
Accountancy	350	0	0	0	0	0	350
Advertising/PR	250	0	0	250	0	0	500
Association fees	100	0	0	0	0	0	100
Bank charges	20	20	20	25	25	25	135
Cleaning – carpets, etc.	20	20	40	20	40	20	160
Commissions paid	0	0	0	0	0	100	100
Ground upkeep	25	25	25	25	25	25	150
Insurance	689	0	0	0	0	0	689
Internet payments	20	20	20	20	20	20	120
Laundry	10	10	10	10	20	20	80
Postage & printing	5	5	5	5	5	5	30
Power	100	100	100	120	120	120	660
Repairs and maintenance	50	50	50	50	50	50	300
Telephone	40	40	40	50	50	50	270
Travelling	50	50	50	100	100	100	450
Vehicle costs	150	150	150	200	200	200	1050
Wages and salaries	0	0	0	200	200	0	400
Sundry	100	100	100	150	150	150	750
Total operating costs	1979	590	610	1225	1005	885	6294
Net profit – £/€/$	-241	1148	1515	1286	2085	1820	7613

Note: Depreciation estimates are not included.

14

Cash flow

The cash-flow chart below looks at my ability to pay bills after food &
provisions. Opening income starts with £2500 seed capital.

Item	Month 1	Month 2	Month3	Month4	Month5	Month6
Opening bank balance	2500	2677	4243	6168	8057	10,885
+ Gross income	2156	2156	2535	3114	3833	3344
– Total operating expenditure	1979	590	610	1225	1005	885
Closing bank balance	2677	4243	6168	8057	10,885	13,344

15

In the cash-flow chart below I have included the cost of sales, purchase of assets, loan repayments, personal drawings and anticipated taxation payments. We will not be taking any drawings in this first six months of operation. Renovations are not included as they are covered by savings.

Item	Month 1	Month 2	Month3	Month4	Month5	Month6
INCOME						
Total Sales – £/€/$	2874	2874	3513	4152	5110	4472
EXPENDITURE						
Purchases	250	0	0	0	0	0
Direct costs	719	719	878	1038	1278	1118
Running/operating costs	2979	590	610	1225	1005	885
Loan repayments	250	250	250	250	250	250
Asset purchases	0	0	0	0	0	1000
Taxation	0	0	0	0	0	750
Other	0	0	0	0	0	0
Total expenditure	**3889**	**1250**	**1544**	**2296**	**2281**	**3843**
Opening balance	2500	253	645	1838	2826	4650
Plus total income	**2874**	**2874**	**3513**	**4152**	**5110**	**4472**
Less total expenditure	253	645	1838	2826	4650	4639
Closing bank balance	**253**	**645**	**1838**	**2826**	**4650**	**4639**

Note: First month's opening balance represents a £€$2500 loan that we have taken out.

At the end of our first four months of operation, we will be developing a three-year business plan that will reflect the experience gained from running a bed & breakfast.

16 Glossary

Account Balance   The difference between the total debits and total credits of an account.

À la Carte   Where the guest can order anything on a menu and only pays for what she/he eats.

Artwork   This is the name given to original material, photographs, illustrations, typesetting (lettering), etc., when making up the overall design of a printing job.

Assets   Thing of value owned by a person or business.

Bad Debt   A loss caused by the failure of a customer to pay for what is owed.

Balance Sheet   A statement at a certain date, setting out the assets, liabilities and proprietorship of a business.

Bookkeeping   The systematic recording of financial transactions in a journal. This could incorporate a trial balance.

Camera Ready Artwork   Artwork prepared to a standard from which images can be created.

Capital   The wealth, including money and property, owned by a person or business.

Commission   Percentage of sale paid as a fee in certain business transactions, e.g. to an agent selling your accommodation.

Cost of Goods Sold   The cost of producing, converting or acquiring goods sold during a period.

Cover   Place or setting at a table. Term used by waiting staff.

Creditor   One to whom money is owed by your business.

Debtor   One who owes money to your business.

Expenditure   Costs and charges of operating a business.

Franchise   A contract under which a party is licensed by another to use a name, product, service or business system, in return for a fee.

Goodwill   An intangible asset which includes business reputation, an established trading level, favourable location, licensing or exclusive trading rights.

HTML   Hyper Text Mark-up Language.

Inbound Tourism   Travellers who are coming to your country from overseas.

Industrial Award   Terms and conditions of employment negotiated and agreed on by employers, government and union representatives.

Invoice   Document showing details of the charges for goods sold or service provided on account.

Invoicing Period   A regular time period after which invoices are issued for all sales made or services provided during that period, normally seven or thirty days.

Journal	A book of first entry in which financial transactions are entered as they occur.
Ledger	A book in which financial transactions are classified in various accounts.
Liabilities	Amounts owed by a person or business, including loans and outstanding debts.
Outbound Tourism	Travellers who reside in your country and are leaving for overseas for their holiday.
Owner's Equity	The value of the person after liabilities have been deducted from assets. This is the amount of money that would be distributed to the owners if the business entity was dissolved.
Rack e	The price at which you advertise your bed & breakfast.
Revenue	Income from business transactions.
Table d'Hôte	A set menu at a set price.
Trading Hours	The time an establishment is open for business.
Trading Terms	The terms of business applied to creditors, e.g. invoices due for payment within seven days of issue.
VAT/GST	Value Added Tax/Goods and Services Tax.
Working Capital	The capital or assets required to fund the daily operation of the business. It is calculated by deducting current liabilities from current assets.

Index

Stewart Whyte

EARN MONEY FROM YOUR HOME

With short lets through Airbnb, Onefinestay, TripAdvisor, Misterbnb and other sites

Earn Money From Your Home

With short lets through Airbnb, Onefinestay, TripAdvisor, Misterbnb and other sites

Stewart Whyte

ISBN: 978-1-47213-773-9

With the growth of online reservation platforms such as Airbnb, TripAdvisor, Wimdu, Booking.com and Onefinestay, people are able to offer accommodation to a huge audience of tourists as B&B hosts or as short break holiday accommodation providers – without using an agent. So earning money from your own home – whether it be letting a few bedrooms in your house, an investment property or a holiday home – has never been easier.

However, to meet the demand and market your accommodation effectively as a host you will need basic knowledge and some professionalism. Good hosts get good reviews, which in turn attract more guests and increase your chances of success and financial reward.

In easy-to-read sections you'll discover:

- **How to get your property ready for a successful listing**
- **The requirements of responsible hosting**
- **How Stayz, Homeaway, mrbnb and other reservation platforms work**
- **How to set your room rate and monitor your bookings**
- **How to market your property internationally and at very little cost.**

This book will explain the issues as they apply to responsible hosting. It will give you the knowledge and confidence to become a successful accommodation provider.

THE
IMPR⟳VEMENT
ZONE

Looking for life inspiration?

The Improvement Zone has it all, from **expert advice** on how to advance your **career** and boost your **business**, to improving your **relationships**, revitalising your **health** and developing your **mind**.

Whatever your goals, head to our website now.

www.improvementzone.co.uk

INSPIRATION ON THE MOVE

INSPIRATION DIRECT TO YOUR INBOX